PRAISE FOR *The Butler Speaks*

"One of my favourite guests, Charles the Butler, gives great advice
on managing your life, loving laundry and pursuing good manners."
MARILYN DENIS
host of *The Marilyn Denis Show* and co-host of *Roger, Darren and Marilyn* on CHUM FM

"Charles the Butler taught me to truly understand what luxury is.
He alone deserves the fifth highly coveted luxury hotel star."
OLIVIER CREMONT
former Head Butler, Fouquet's Barrière Hôtel, Paris

"*The Butler Speaks* is your definitive guide to the art of living well, delivered with
the wit, charm, style—and simple common sense—that you have come to expect
from Charles' columns in *Metro*. Keep it handy and you'll never misstep!"
CHARLOTTE EMPEY
Editor-in-Chief, *Metro* (English Canada)

"Charles has been my go-to resource for nearly a decade now. His expertise, elegance,
and thoughtful tips are an unbeatable combination. I am thrilled that he is sharing
his in-depth knowledge with the public in this handy resource."
BENJAMEN DOUGLAS
former Household Manager to Morgan Freeman and Myrna Colley-Lee

"Not everyone needs, wants or can afford a butler, but anyone who takes pride in their home and in entertaining their family and friends will find within these pages the tips and tricks that a professional butler uses to achieve the ultimate standards of a privately staffed house."

JOHN ROBERTSON

butler to Their Graces the Duke and Duchess of Northumberland, Alnwick Castle

"All warmth and charm, Charles takes the stuffiness out of butlering. When Charles the Butler speaks, I listen! He presents the 'old school' lessons of etiquette, entertaining and housekeeping in a way that everyone can learn. I am proud he is a Master Trainer at my school."

PAMELA EYRING

President, The Protocol School of Washington

"Charles MacPherson reminds us just how powerful and dynamic the personal touch can be in our daily lives and how attention to even the smallest of details can give us an edge—whether we live in small studio apartments or entertain in mansions; whether we wish to connect with a few or impress hundreds. *The Butler Speaks* is a must-have resource, for the corporate executive to the recent university graduate and everyone in between."

CHRIS YOUNG

President, Protocol and Diplomacy International, Protocol Officers Association

Welcome.

CHARLES MacPHERSON

The Butler Speaks

A *Guide to*

STYLISH ENTERTAINING,

ETIQUETTE,

and the Art of

GOOD HOUSEKEEPING

appetite
by RANDOM HOUSE

Appetite by Random House and colophon are registered trademarks.

Library and Archives of Canada Cataloguing in Publication is available upon request.
ISBN: 978-0-449-015919

Book design: CS Richardson
Cover images: © Steve Cukrov/Shutterstock.com, © Jirsak/Shutterstock.com

Illustrations throughout (except for those noted below) by Sean Kelley, courtesy of Charles MacPherson Academy Inc.
iii, 1, 39, 81, 145, 177, 223: © *ImageZoo/Corbis. 68: Hein Nouwens/Shutterstock.com. 84: Aleksei Makarov/Shutterstock.com.*
85, 117, 141: lynea/Shutterstock.com. 87: Roberto Castillo/Shutterstock.com. 103, 151, 158: Antonio Abrignani/
Shutterstock.com. 118: Hein Nouwens/Shutterstock.com. 125: bioraven/Shutterstock.com 152: Igor Kali/Shutterstock.com.
197: chippix/Shutterstock.com. xix, 16, 17, 26 (lower), 29, 35, 36, 37, 51 (lower), 52, 53, 58 (lower), 119, 129,
182, 187 (upper), 188, 195, 201 (upper), 204, 207, and 213 (upper).

PRINTED AND BOUND IN THE USA

Published in Canada by Appetite by Random House,
a division of Random House of Canada Limited
www.randomhouse.ca

10 9 8 7 6 5 4 3 2 1

With much love to the grandmothers of my life,
Gisèle Deleuze, Gretta MacPherson and Simone Mathan,
whose great dignity, grace and style helped mould me into who I am today.

Contents

Foreword

AS THE HEAD BUTLER of the Savoy hotel in London, I have dedicated my life to the pursuit of excellent service. I feel strongly that the best service can be a bridge between cultures and lifestyles, and that good service makes the difference between clients feeling comfortable or ill at ease. In addition to my years spent working in some of the finest hotels in London, I have worked with royal families, and in private homes in Europe and the Middle East. And over these last thirty years that I have been a butler and household manager, there have been numerous changes to my industry. In past years, I was often asked to book a private car or limousine for a client, but I now find myself fielding requests for private jets! Butlering is steeped in tradition, and with change to the service industry happening at a rapid pace, it's easy to see why some people feel that butlers might be a bit out of touch. But competent, contemporary butlers are taking on new roles as lifestyle managers, roles that encompass a wide range of tasks.

by Sean Davoren

In my professional life, I count myself fortunate to have come across Charles MacPherson—a butler whose passion and expertise have reinvigorated the hospitality industry. Charles and I met through our mutual friend and colleague John Robertson. At the time, I was running the butler department at the Lanesborough Hotel, and Charles was preparing to open his school for butlers in North America. That night, as we sat at a bar and enjoyed two bottles of champagne, I learned that Charles is a butler par excellence. He has trained luxury hotel staff around the world and his advice is sought after, not only by people in the industry, but by the general public as well. And now, he's collected his wisdom in this incredibly helpful book.

If you've encountered Charles before, you'll know that he has a unique ability to translate the traditions of butlering for a modern audience. But what is most admirable about Charles is his consummate professionalism. When we first met, even as we "talked shop," Charles was the epitome of discretion, never divulging the names of his clients and always conversing in a way that assumed dignity and respect for the service industry. *The Butler Speaks* is a culmination of Charles' marvellous enthusiasm for and expertise in butlering. He offers guidance that is not only for owners of lavish estates or fans of *Downton Abbey* but for anyone who wants to live with grace and style. What Charles does so well is show us that the principles of butlering are accessible to all— whether you rent a small urban condo or own a large home. *The Butler Speaks* covers the essentials of proper etiquette, entertaining, and household management, and provides tips that are applicable to both your personal and professional life. In this day and age, specific protocol can sometimes seem fussy and irrelevant; however, now more than ever, the art of service is an imperative skill. Charles has delivered a book with all the flair, charm and unpretentious grace of a true butler.

Introduction

WE LIVE IN A TIME when technology is taking over our lives. We used to spend every evening breaking bread with friends and family at the dinner table, but the demands of modern living are such that, for many of us, dinner is picked up from a drive-through window while rushing to a kid's soccer practice. Home entertainment is more about microwaved popcorn and a movie rental, and housekeeping is that Sunday afternoon scramble to do laundry and tidy up before another busy workweek begins. Similarly, rules of social decorum have fallen by the wayside, and fewer people seem to realize the true value of proper etiquette and how it can enrich our daily lives and social interactions. Though we are lucky to have so many amenities at our fingertips, never before has there been a time when we needed professional guidance more—on manners and etiquette, on how to entertain with style and on how to manage our homes in a way that provides greater quality of life and results in happiness. My goal in writing this book is to share my experience in household

Stay professional and you will never go wrong.

management and butlering, and in doing so offer to you, dear reader, all manner of knowledge to help you run your own household the way a good butler would—with class, poise and care.

Many people feel that having proper manners means being stuffy and pretentious, but I'm here to tell you that nothing could be further from the truth! You can be well-mannered, cultured and a great home entertainer while being yourself—in fact, there's no other way to be. For me, etiquette is not a set of classist rules for rich, famous or snobby people—rather, it's a way of being based on understanding other people and having consideration for their needs. Letitia Baldrige (1925–2012), one of the grand dames of American etiquette, once told me her definition of *etiquette*. She defined it as how we act at the breakfast table when sitting with family; how we speak to the bus driver on our way to work; or how we speak to someone like our mother-in-law when she is driving us a little crazy. What she was suggesting is that etiquette applies to everyone—in any social interaction. Forget memorizing rigid Victorian rules and outdated codes of conduct. Modern-day etiquette is about behaving with grace around others and having confidence in yourself while doing so. Etiquette has another function as well. Knowledge of good manners gives us something to fall back on in new, strange or awkward situations. Good etiquette always takes into account cultural, generational and social differences and allows people to handle all situations with civility and dignity.

I have served as major-domo for prominent families around the world, offering household help and staff training services in countless countries. It is my belief that there is no political or business leader, dignitary, king or queen, or movie star who can manage without domestic professionals in the wings. The need for good household service professionals is so great that in 2009 I launched a new school, the Charles MacPherson Academy for Butlers and Household Managers. It is the only registered school for butlers and household managers in North America, and my mission, as founder, is to offer excellent education to prepare household staff for the service industry.

Etiquette is not a set of classical rules for the rich, famous or snobby—rather, it's a way of understanding other people and having consideration for their needs.

What a really good butler knows are the secrets of the trade that simplify housekeeping and entertaining at home. It's the little luxuries—simple human kindness, decency and attention to detail—that make a dinner memorable or that turn a house into a home. *The Butler Speaks* is a reference guide that will simplify your life and help you take pleasure in the small luxuries available to all of us. Because no matter who you are, you can lead a more productive social life (and a more productive career too) with tips and tricks learned from a professional butler.

I consider myself lucky indeed to have worked in my profession for more than twenty-four years. I have had the opportunity to watch the most incredible events unfold within the walls of famous and luxurious households around the world. How many people get the chance to witness a dinner in the state dining room of Buckingham

Palace? Or stay in the private residence of the renowned Hôtel du Marc, owned by Veuve Clicquot Ponsardin? Or spend hours flying at 35,000 feet in a Gulfstream v with a celebrity? Butlers and household managers work hard, but in return, we are offered a rare glimpse of the daily lives of the rich and famous.

But perhaps you're wondering what that has to do with you. As busy working people, you and I have many demands and stresses on our personal and professional lives that we need to overcome. That's where I come in. Just as you would seek medical or legal help for a problem, I am the professional who has insight into how to make entertaining, manners and housekeeping a natural part of your life. These skills are the competitive advantages the rich and famous use every day, and you can use them too.

To truly understand the importance of service, we must first understand its history. Household management has existed in some form or other since the first homes and palaces were built centuries ago. The organizational structure of household management as we know it today is relatively new, but even the new borrows from the past.

In 1827, one of the first books on household management was published by Robert Roberts (1777–1860). Entitled *The House Servant's Directory*, it was also one of the first books ever published by an African American. In it, Roberts, a butler for the senator and governor of Massachusetts, offered valuable information for servants not only on how to perform household duties but also on proper and professional behaviour. His common-sense approach to household management is still relevant today, even though modern technologies have changed the way the home is run and cleaned.

Later, renowned French chef Auguste Escoffier (1846–1935) took the next step in revolutionizing the kitchen. He is credited with bringing order and efficiency to the hotel kitchen the likes of which had never been seen before. For the first time, the staff members in Escoffier's kitchens were organized into teams. Each team was responsible for a production station and all the teams reported to the executive chef—and because this method was so successful commercially, it trickled down to become an integral part of household management. Today, all large households maintain many of the principles of staff organization, and this is true of the whole staff, not just the kitchen staff.

Just as the kitchen was becoming organized in France, so too was the Victorian aristocratic household in Britain. This new interest in a better-functioning home led to the publication of several important books on household management. In 1861, the revolutionary Mrs. Isabella Beeton (1836–1865) wrote *Mrs. Beeton's Book of Household Management*. This unique reference book was among the first to formalize job duties within a household and to teach both technique and best practices of modern household management. Before Mrs. Beeton, aristocrats and servants ran large homes and estates with whatever knowledge they had gained from personal experience, but no written compendium had collected the practices of the domestic trade. This was a how-to book more complete than anything previously published, and at 1,112 pages including

Cover of the first edition of *Mrs. Beeton's Book of Household Management*, 1861.

900 recipes, it was an overwhelmingly detailed reference for its time.

Following in the footsteps of the formidable Mrs. Beeton was Charles Pierce, who, in 1863, wrote one of my favourite books, *The Household Manager*. *The Court Journal* described so accurately why this book was important: "This work explains in a very clear and business-like way the management of a first-class household where a regular set of servants is kept. It will be found highly useful to those who desire information on this subject." What *The Household Manager* did, in my opinion, was legitimize the service profession, putting emphasis on the craft and skills a butler or other household professional needed to run an estate.

I strongly believe that many of the principles and methods first established by Roberts, Beeton and Pierce are as important today as they ever were. The basic methodology of household management has not changed and need not change. A bed is made the same way it always was—with a bottom and top sheet; however, new linen technologies and the quality of blankets have improved dramatically. Similarly, we clean our bathrooms the way we always have, but new products and modern plumbing lend ease to the task. Finally, serving at table remains as it has for centuries, with various methods in use (such as silver service, Russian service and plate service), but the style and variety of tableware has evolved. As a butler and as a teacher, I want to help you keep the traditions of yesteryear but use modern techniques and tools that will make managing your home simpler and more efficient.

Household management has finally come of age, and seasoned professionals who work in the industry have garnered respect for their profession, respect that unfortunately was not always accorded to the domestic servants who came before them. Charwomen, scullery maids, hallboys, footmen—these workers and others like them were once considered by many to be low in status and they certainly did not earn the salaries they deserved for the hard work they did. But there's now a newfound respect shown for the true housekeeping professional, which is why I like to repeat my motto to all the apprentices I train at my butler school: "Stay professional and you will never go wrong." This is as true for the butler as it is for you, dear reader. Treat your home, your guests and your colleagues with professionalism, and you can never go wrong.

The domestic industry has given me many golden opportunities. I have worked with world leaders, organized dinners for captains of industry, and trained corporations and luxury hotel staff on proper conduct and entertaining. I have even had the chance in the home of a celebrity client to hold in my hands an Oscar statuette. (I made sure to polish it properly before returning it, gleaming, to its shelf!) I often think how lucky I am, Charles MacPherson, born in Fort William, Canada, to be able to work in such a fascinating milieu. I firmly believe that the domestic industry is a profession to be proud of and that keeping the protocols of both the past and the present alive in today's household is an art. Fortunately, it's an art that can be learned, and learning it will lend simple grace and beauty to your life.

The famous designer Oscar de la Renta taught me one of the most important lessons of my professional life. When asked, "What is luxury?" His response was this: "Luxury is a feeling." He went on to explain that paying a high price to be served a cup of coffee in a fancy hotel by an employee who pays no attention to you is *not* luxury because it doesn't make you feel special; rather, you leave disappointed. In contrast, buying a cheaper coffee prepared by a street vendor who gives you his undivided attention makes you feel important and welcome. That is good service. That *is* luxury.

Luxury can be had by anyone, because it's about giving someone the gift of feeling welcomed, cherished and looked after. This is the essence of my book, one that I hope you will enjoy from start to finish.

Charles P. MacPherson

Part One

The Tradition of Service

MANY PEOPLE EQUATE the Victorian and Edwardian eras with beauty, grace and luxury, and it's true that they were splendid times—if you belonged to the upper classes, those privileged few who could afford to live opulently because a vast subservient class supported their every need and fancy. I think what people often forget is the amount of effort it took to create that surface elegance we associate with late-19th- and early-20th-century Britain.

Consider the analogy of a beautiful swan on a lake. The swan is a gorgeous sight to behold, white and supremely magnificent against a backdrop of lush green. She's a vision of poise and beauty as she glides effortlessly across the water's surface. But, in fact, what we don't see when we admire her are her powerful webbed feet pedalling furiously underneath her. It takes all of that hidden raw energy and effort for her to move gracefully across the water. And that is exactly what the majority of the population in England was doing for those very few people living a grand lifestyle in

Victorian and Edwardian times. All of those workers were the undercarriage of the swan, and those precious few aristocrats floated luxuriously on the surface.

And so, what looked like a picture of grace wasn't really an easy lifestyle to uphold! It's not as though the privileged classes could, as we do today, run to the local store and buy dinner pre-made. In the past, it was actually *hard* to produce a meal—the swan's feet had to churn at top speed to achieve it. Everything had to be made from scratch; and although as a consequence of the Industrial Revolution mass-produced household goods were starting to become a reality, they were still limited, by today's standard of convenience. Remember, too, that in the middle of the 19th century, these grand estates did not have electricity, hot running water, efficient plumbing or central heating, so for members of the aristocracy to live comfortably, large domestic staffs were needed. The households of the wealthy were cleaned from top to bottom, and the chemicals employed were harsh and damaging to human health (though few knew it then). Days would start with chambermaids having to light fires in bedrooms long before their well-to-do and well-rested occupants woke up. Heaven forbid her ladyship should rise with cold feet. Scullery maids would carry heavy buckets of coal from the basement up numerous flights of narrow stairs. And that was even before the food preparation or cleaning was done! Dozens of service people were involved in presenting just one perfect meal in a spotlessly clean and aesthetically pleasing dining room. Life for the service class was hard, very hard, and servants regularly worked seventeen hours per day, six and a half days per week!

So, while we romanticize the poetic beauty and civility of these eras of extravagance, it's all too easy to forget just how much service was required to support so few living in a state of grandeur. According to the occupation census of England and Wales (1851 and 1861), domestic employees were the second-largest category of workers, outnumbered only by agricultural workers, who were also largely employed by grand estates. And by 1871, for the first time in history, the domestic working class had grown by 21 percent, making it the largest group of employees in Great Britain.

As the 19th century drew to a close, so too did the Victorian era and the class divide between upstairs and downstairs started to change. Investment in estate farming was down significantly and food and goods from abroad were cheaper to import than to make on home soil. Those with means began to shift their wealth from agriculture to the banking and financial worlds. The vast mansions of the

---

THE BUTLER'S TOOLKIT: WHITE GLOVES

Through the early 20th century, butlers didn't wear white gloves—only footmen did. White gloves were used to set a table so that the footman's fingerprints didn't smudge the plates. Once a footman graduated to a higher level of service as a butler, he didn't need to use white gloves anymore. Today, however, the opposite is true. The higher the status of a household, the more common is white glove service. If a butler is going to carry gloves, he always carries them in his left hand, with his right hand behind his back.

---

past century became too costly to run, both because of the labour required to keep them afloat and because of a lack of modernization. King Edward's rise to the throne in 1901 to reign over the United Kingdom, the British Dominions and India coincided with a new era of modernization and socialism, both of which marked the beginning of the end of an entire way of life.

The Edwardian era saw domestic staff leaving en masse the estates where they'd worked for much of their lives. They were pursuing dreams of a better and more independent life, going to work in the factories of the newly industrialized world. Servant women put down their coal buckets and scullery implements to take up typewriters and pursue secretarial duties. For a while, this shift caused a labour crisis, as women eschewed the work they'd done for decades in private service and sought new career ventures. As the First World War loomed and finally descended upon the world, the domestic industry was devastated. Men left their jobs on private estates to go to war, where many were either tragically killed or wounded. Those who were able returned home looking for emerging opportunities in industry or manufacturing. In fact, this moment marks a critical turning point: going forward, domestic work would be done primarily by women, and few men would be employed in private service.

As the 20th century progressed and the Second World War drew to a close, the 1950s ushered in further seismic changes to the tradition of service. The expanded middle class with its new purchasing power could suddenly afford to buy goods and products of its own, instead of relying on the beneficence (or lack thereof) of its wealthy employers. Consumerism was the dawn of a new era of convenience, with fast food, cheap clothing, automobiles and air transportation available if not to all, then at least to many more. Relatively few people remained employed in domestic service, and the traditions of an era were beginning to be replaced by a faster, mechanized route to household management.

By the mid-1960s—the era of "free love"—one hundred years after such a strict and oppressed time, the rules of social decorum and manners had become more relaxed than ever. Formal entertaining with a domestic staff was rare or non-existent; written invitations and thank-you notes were from a time gone by; and mass-produced food became a staple in most households. The pendulum had definitely swung the other way. By the '70s and '80s, however, the pendulum had swung yet again, and even as every middle-class household now had access to consumer goods (vacuums, washers, dryers) that made cleaning and cooking more manageable, for a few with means, a return to the tradition of service could be had. Ronald Reagan became president of the United States and Margaret Thatcher presided over Great Britain. Huge amounts of wealth were being made on two continents, and suddenly, newly minted millionaires and billionaires began building large estates, like their ancestors from a century earlier. The demand for trained domestic staff suddenly increased, but the Western world lacked a work-force trained for these jobs.

THE BUTLER'S TOOLKIT: THE BUTLER'S BOOK

The butler of the Victorian era established many of the skills and methodologies that are practised by the household manager today. A perfect example is the book kept by the butler to record all things related to the home. Staff and maintenance schedules; inventory of china, cutlery and glassware; personal family information, such as food preferences, allergies and clothing sizes—all of this information was catalogued in a traditional butler's book. The household procedures manual is the modern-day version.

In 1981, Mr. Ivor Spencer opened the Ivor Spencer International School for Butler Administrators and Personal Assistants in London. The school began in a modest way, in a church basement, but it offered what no one had offered before: proper education and training for individuals who were not "to the manor born" and who wished to dedicate their lives to domestic service. Remember that the majority of the rich no longer had personal butlers, so the art of butlering was on the verge of being lost. With this renaissance in butlering and household management came a newfound respect for the profession. Domestic service was no longer seen as an occupation held exclusively by the lower classes but as a decent and honourable profession that required true skill and talent. The remuneration for such work rose accordingly, as domestic workers and their employers realized the value of their efforts. Since the opening of Ivor's school, others have come and gone, but only a few remain as true professional schools with proper accreditation and educational affiliations.

Today, we are fascinated by the idea of service, by the notion of having a class of other people who look after our every need and whim. Look no further than the popularity of shows such as *Downton Abbey* and *Upstairs, Downstairs*, and you will see reflected in them our own curiosity about a way of life that has largely been relegated to the past, even if the tradition of service remains strong to this day. Regardless of our fascination with what is a bygone era, what remains true—and will remain true forever—is that there will always be a need for good service professionals, for people who know how to behave with grace and classic style, and how to make a household run smoothly and seamlessly, no matter what its size. That is the real tradition of service, and its legacy lives on.

COMMON JOBS IN THE EDWARDIAN HOUSEHOLD

On the next page is a list of typical job titles and duties from the Edwardian era. Each estate would have slightly different duties and expectations for its workers, but by and large, these roles were the same throughout the United Kingdom

Maids   Valet Lady's   Butler Head   Underbutlers/   Maids
                      maid   housekeeper   Footmen

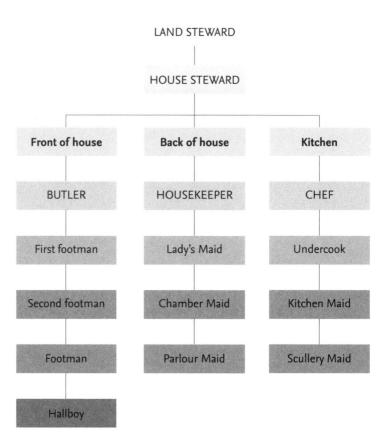

LAND STEWARD
|
HOUSE STEWARD

Front of house	Back of house	Kitchen
BUTLER	HOUSEKEEPER	CHEF
First footman	Lady's Maid	Undercook
Second footman	Chamber Maid	Kitchen Maid
Footman	Parlour Maid	Scullery Maid
Hallboy		

The Edwardian Household

and beyond. There were three branches of domestic service—the front of house, the back of house and the kitchen. Front of house refers to servants who could be seen by guests: these were servants of higher rank. Back of the house servants would almost never be seen by the family or by guests. If the estate had neither a land steward nor a house steward, the butler was the head of the front of the house; the housekeeper the head of the back of the house; and the chef the head of the kitchen. These three employees served as managers, and staff within each branch reported to them. Sometimes the chef would report to the housekeeper rather than to the house steward, depending on the household.

LAND STEWARD

This highly educated gentleman was responsible for managing the estate profitably. He was the highest-paid employee living on the estate and was considered above all other servants in station.

HOUSE STEWARD

This gentleman kept track of spending and was responsible for all purchases made for the estate. He reported to the land steward and owners. He was also responsible for hiring, firing and paying out all salaries for the domestic staff. Today, this role is called the head of human resources.

BUTLER

By the Edwardian era, the butler was the highest-ranking official within a household staff. He was responsible for running the household, and all male staff members reported to him directly. His primary duties included overseeing all functions and events held in the drawing room (known today as the living room) and the dining room, and overseeing the front door and the wine cellar. A parlour maid and pantry maid were assigned to these areas to keep rooms immaculately clean. He was responsible for all visual and service aspects within the dining and drawing room areas, including ensuring silver was polished. The British butler was present at breakfast, but served only lunch and dinner.

FIRST FOOTMAN

This individual reported to the butler and was in training to one day be a household butler himself. His duties extended outside the household and first footmen could often be seen accompanying the lady of the house on shopping excursions. The first footman assisted the butler with serving at mealtimes. Interestingly, the man in this position was paid based on his beauty and height rather than on his abilities. The taller and more handsome he was, the more money he made! For the rich, this servant was a powerful status symbol.

SECOND FOOTMAN

Working under the first footman, this man was in training to continue moving up the domestic service ladder. His job duties were similar to those of the first footman and, just like him, his salary was determined both by his height and personal attractiveness.

FOOTMAN

A man in this low-status position would assist the other footmen and the butler with opening doors, serving at the table and any other duties as instructed by those of higher rank.

HALLBOY

This entry-level position in the household was considered the lowest held by a man within an estate. This young man was so low in rank that he wasn't even given a room, but instead slept in the hallway of the back of the house. He was at the beck and call of others almost twenty-four hours a day, and was given the worst chores and tasks.

HOUSEKEEPER

There was a time when the housekeeper was the most powerful domestic servant within the household—the reason being that she held all the household and larder keys. By the Edwardian era, however, she assumed a slightly lesser role within the household, though she was still the head of all female staff. The housekeeper was responsible for controlling all household stores, handing out supplies for the day to the staff, keeping count and control of household linens, inspecting the work of the maids and mending clothing. Although it is a very old custom, some British homes still operate with the housekeeper as the head of the domestic staff and manageress of the residence.

LADY'S MAID

The main purpose of the lady's maid was to be both companion and private maid to the lady of the household. The lady's maid usually reported to the lady of the house directly. She was responsible for all the clothing and grooming of the lady of the house. As such, she often had a particularly close relationship with her employer. It was imperative that she have an excellent grasp of language and be able to converse at a high level with her employer. She was highly literate, and some lady's maids even performed basic secretarial duties. Sadly for her, the typical lady's maid had a hard time fitting in. She was somewhat in limbo, not fully part of the

upstairs world and yet rarely trusted by the downstairs staff.
This meant she was often isolated and lonely.

CHAMBER MAID

The chamber maid's job was to clean and maintain the
private bedrooms of the household. Although chamber
maids were not supposed to have relationships with the
family, because of the nature of their job and the fact that
their duties required them to be in the same rooms as family
members, they sometimes became closer to the family than
to other domestic workers. This accorded them privileges
and benefits that other workers did not have. Being a
chamber maid was very hard work, as she was responsible
for carrying heavy buckets of hot and cold water up the
servants' stairs for family members' private baths. One bath
could require as much as forty-five gallons of water, and it
was an enormous strain to carry it up staircases, through
hallways and into the various private bedrooms of the
house's occupants.

PARLOUR MAID

She would begin her day at the crack of dawn by sweeping
and dusting the drawing room, dining room, library, front
hall and sitting rooms, as well as lighting all of the fires in
these rooms. She would clean lamps, polish silver and keep
the rooms looking tidy, all the while never being seen and
never speaking unless spoken to first. If her employers—or
anyone else, for that matter—entered a room while she was
working, she would discreetly slip away.

CHEF

It was most prestigious for families of the Edwardian era to have a French chef working in the household. Meals were elaborate and presentation was most important in order to impress visitors and guests. The chef put together the menus of the household and was responsible for the food budget. The chef also supervised the execution of meals and all kitchen staff. Although some households had female cooks, such as Mrs. Patmore on the television series *Downton Abbey*, most chefs were men.

UNDERCOOK

Known today as a "sous chef," this person worked directly under the chef and was in training to one day hold his prestigious job. Undercooks worked very hard, as did everyone else in the kitchen.

THE BUTLER'S TOOLKIT: THE RED BOX

The Queen of England receives daily from her private secretary a locked "red box." This box contains official papers from Her Majesty's Government for her review. Most of these documents require Royal Assent in the form of her signature before they can become law.

When I was in private service, written communication between my employer and me was critical; however, the amount of mail and communication from other sources such as my employer's office and charities meant that sometimes my communication would not be reviewed for several days or weeks. To solve this problem, I began putting my regular communication to my employer in a red envelope. My red envelope was always visible on my employer's desk and clearly from me, and I found that I would generally get the answers I was seeking within twenty-four hours.

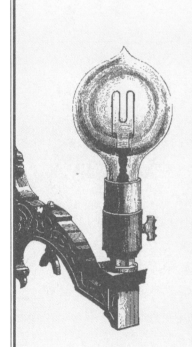

BEFORE THOMAS EDISON had his first successful test of a functioning light bulb on October 22, 1879, the world of the manor house was a different place. Homes were lit using candles and kerosene lanterns. Can you imagine all the work involved for domestic staff, who had to maintain the lanterns, keeping the wicks trimmed and the bases filled at all times? And can you imagine the smoke and dust created by the candles and lanterns? And guess who had to clean all that dirt. So one would think that the response to the invention of the light bulb would be exclamations of "Eureka!" No more dirt, right? No more fuss? No more fire hazards? Everyone should have been thrilled and excited— but, alas, that wasn't quite the way it happened.

When electricity made it into fine homes and estates, people were afraid of it—and not just the staff, the estate owners as well. They feared that electricity gave off invisible harmful "vapours" and that these unseen beasties were dangerous to human health (unlike, say, kerosene burned indoors throughout the winter with no ventilation!). For a while, these fears slowed the acceptance of electricity into homes. Thankfully, a light bulb eventually went on (figuratively speaking and literally) and people realized that electricity was safe and would make everyday life easier and better. It was expensive to install; however, homes and factories ultimately were outfitted with this modern convenience.

The introduction of electricity changed domestic service significantly, and it also led to a reduction of staff within Edwardian estates because not as much physical labour was needed to keep a home running. Electricity allowed for the invention of tools that saved time and energy. Here is an example: Imagine the amount of labour and time required for someone in the kitchen to make whipped cream by hand for a dessert for twenty-four people. Have you ever tried whipping even *one cup* of cream by hand? You need biceps of steel, and many arms. Now compare that to the amount of labour and time it takes to do the same task with an electric mixer. Suddenly whipped cream for twenty-four is easy.

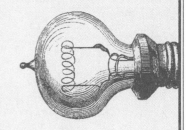

Think of all these kinds of small household tasks and how much more efficient servants could be with electric tools and you'll understand also how human power was becoming less necessary. Even as servants who kept their jobs had a slightly easier time of it, household staff generally suffered the consequences of the invention of electricity in the form of lost employment. Electricity in the home signalled the dawn of a new age, but in some ways it was also a harbinger of the fall of the service industry, which was yet to come.

KITCHEN MAID

The kitchen maid was responsible for keeping the kitchen clean for the chef and undercook. Kitchen maids lit the fires and kept the stove and ovens burning. They did all the grunt work and food preparation required for meals, including cleaning vegetables and peeling potatoes.

SCULLERY MAID

This entry-level position in the household was considered the lowest position held by women. Consequently it was one of the worst jobs. It was usually done by a woman who was young and uneducated. Scullery maids washed dishes, pots and pans all day. The hours were long, pay was low and other domestic workers accorded them almost no respect. Apart from the hard labour involved, their duties required them to use cleaning agents of the era that were harsh on the skin and often toxic. A scullery maid could rise through the ranks, but even the most ambitious and lucky could aspire only to a position as maid working in the front of the house.

HOUSEHOLD STAFF GREETING LINE

A few years ago, a client asked me to go to his country residence to spend some time training the staff. My client's residence has been in the family for several generations and is particularly large, even by my standards, and they have almost two hundred people on staff. In fact, I don't think I have ever worked in a bigger household! While I was there, my client asked me if I could train the household staff in the tradition of the staff greeting line. This is a formal reception whereby the house staff gathers in an organized manner outside the house to greet guests upon their arrival and to bid them farewell when they are leaving. Those of you who watch *Downton Abbey* will have seen the household staff line up at the main entrance of Highclere Castle whenever a new guest is scheduled to arrive.

Well, I must admit, at first I had no idea how to set up a staff greeting line. It's not a task that modern household managers have to see to very often! And I had never done it before, though of course I'd seen it in movies and on TV, like everyone else. I had to think about it for a moment. Could I pull this off? How would I organize such a display? And would it make any sense in a modern context? Suddenly the answers came to me: it was simple logic! Of course I could recreate the staff greeting line in a contemporary setting. The organizational principle was the same as it always had been: I would use the "order of precedence" and rank staff according to seniority in the line, just as they do in diplomatic circles when presenting a dignitary.

STAFF GREETING LINE

To form a greeting line, the staff is arranged in a single line, standing side by side (or "shoulder to shoulder" in the parlance of household management). Traditionally, the most senior employee is closest to the front door and the most junior closest to the arriving guests. The greeting line is always on a forty-five-degree angle so that as guests approach the front door the staff are progressively closer to them. Staff members are to stand with their hands behind their backs. Subliminally, this is so that guests won't feel obliged to shake every employee's hand, which would make for a rather slow and awkward process.

If you ever happen to be on the receiving end of a staff greeting line, remember that you need only walk up to the front door to meet your host or hostess, who will welcome you to the residence—there is no need to greet everyone along the way. Sometimes the butler will be introduced, and in that case you may say a simple "good afternoon."

Here's something I learned when I had to recreate the staff greeting line for my client: this must have been a difficult ritual to pull off in the Edwardian era because there were no cell phones! When I had to do it, I could communicate by phone with the drivers who were escorting the guests to the home, and I could post a watch at the end of the road to alert me when the cars were approaching the main driveway. How this was done in the past, how the timing was coordinated so that the staff wasn't waiting outside for hours, I have no idea.

LIFE "DOWNSTAIRS"

In the Victorian and Edwardian eras, the primary reason why people went into private service was to gain easy access to daily fresh food and shelter. The class divide was extreme in Great Britain, and many people would not have been able to afford housing or sufficient food without working for a wealthy landowner. There was no safety net of any kind, especially for the poor, and the world was a tough place for those who had to survive on their own. As challenging as domestic life may have been, the reward was that if you did your job well and took pride in your work, you would always have a roof over your head and food in your belly.

The work ethic of the past was different from today's. The notion of leisure time is really a modern one, and workers of past eras were expected to spend most of their waking lives serving the household. Life was strict and harsh. A worker caught in the wrong area of the house for no good reason would most certainly be dismissed immediately—without a reference, which severely compromised their chances of ever obtaining gainful employment again.

The downstairs is where servants spent most of their working lives. The front-of-house staff would have access to the well-appointed upstairs rooms, but the back-of-house staff rarely caught a glimpse of what the upstairs looked liked. The family upstairs rarely ventured downstairs. Occasionally, the lady of the house might go below in search of a servant, but her husband was never seen downstairs. It's as though each floor—upstairs and down—was its own separate universe, and only on a few occasions did the two converge in any way.

One of these occasions was the yearly servants' ball, which many traditional households held as a way to thank staff for their work. At the annual staff ball, upstairs residents danced and socialized with downstairs staff in a way that was permitted only on that day. This was a lovely meeting of the two worlds, which at its best engendered respect between staff and family. This tradition is still preserved on some older and formal estates in Britain, though of course it has changed a little over time, just as the status and role of domestic service has changed.

As for the geography of downstairs, the ceilings were low and the rooms small and functional. During the day and well into the evening, the downstairs was full of much hustle and bustle, as servants moved through the hallways to the various rooms where the tools of their trade were kept. Each room served a specific purpose, such as a small room used specifically for polishing shoes, or one devoted to polishing silver.

The staff usually ate together in a staff dining room. In most residences, the staff dining room was not a grand space like the dining room upstairs, but rather austere, with an imposing, solid table in the centre (though some grand houses had grand staff dining rooms as well). Everyone would have known their place at the table and each servant would sit according to rank. The butler sat at the head of the table, with the lowest-ranking staff member—usually the scullery maid—at the other end. On the right of the butler, the housekeeper would find her place, and on his left would sit the lady's maid. The first footman and second footman would be next, and all servants would then follow according to their rank, but alternating male and female.

The one good thing about being in service was the guarantee of food. While others not in the employ of an estate struggled every day to feed themselves, domestic staff could count on a fairly good diet and three square meals a day. Before the Second World War, in good houses it was tradition that the staff actually ate the same meal that the family ate upstairs. (This lovely tradition is sometimes continued in fine houses today.)

The chef prepared the meals for upstairs and for downstairs, and the front-of-house servants usually left the upstairs once the cocktail hour began and had their meal downstairs while the family upstairs got slightly tipsy. The downstairs meal was a "host serves" meal, meaning that the butler would plate the food, apportioning each worker their share. Interestingly, the cooks and the cooking staff would rarely eat at the servants' dining table; instead, they would take their meals in the kitchen, among staff of their own rank and division.

The only time the men and women were able to socialize was at the table, or on occasions when the butler and the lady of the house approved a dance or social gathering, which always took place downstairs. Otherwise, men and women were expected to keep their distance and carry on social relationships only with the same sex. Occasionally, staff would take their chores to the dining room table—for instance, when mending a sock (nothing was disposable like it is today!)—so that they'd have a moment of permitted social interaction with the opposite sex. Also, the dining room was more comfortable and provided a larger workspace than did the staff living quarters. In this way, it served for the staff almost the same function as a modern living room.

Gossip was discouraged by the head servants, but inevitable, and it was traded like a kind of currency among staff members. Information was power, and because the downstairs staff often lacked authority, gossip was a way of understanding the inner workings of the household and of using that knowledge to jockey for advantage.

The butler and the housekeeper had their own residences, which were usually in the basement, whereas the rest of the servants had quarters upstairs in the attic. The butler and housekeeper's rooms were larger than those of other staff and more comfortable. They usually had a fireplace—a luxury when you consider how cold the manor house must have been. So why were these two positions housed in the basement? The idea was that by being near the operational rooms (and the wine cellar, in particular!) the butler and housekeeper could keep an eye at all times on the household provisions and supplies.

Meanwhile, in the attic, workers shared, usually two to a bedroom. In order for staff to get to their rooms in the attic, both the men and the women would use the servants' staircases at the back of the house. These were private, narrow staircases—often one for the men, one for the women—and everything from the downstairs was ferried up step by painful step. The bedrooms were spartan and utilitarian, including a bed, a dresser and some sort of religious Christian item, like a cross on the wall. The women usually even shared a bed. Can you imagine knowing you'd get only a few hours' sleep before you'd have to be up again at the crack of dawn, slaving away at your very physically demanding job? And on top of that to have to share a bed with a cranky cook who kept you up with her horrible snoring? It was not a glamorous life.

You'll recall that I said most servants worked six and a half days every week. Why just a half-day off, not a full day? Because staff were required to maintain the same religious practice and faith as the family upstairs. If the family ordained that you should kneel at the pew, you kneeled at the pew. And that took up the better part of your "day off."

Consider, too, that there was often only one bathroom within the entire men's living quarters, and the same was true for the women's. You were expected to get in, take care of business and get out again quickly. Most houses maintained additional rules about bathing. In some houses, staff had to bathe once a week—whether they needed to or not! It's hard to imagine that servants would have maintained high standards of personal hygiene. I often imagine—with little sense of wonder or nostalgia—just how bad they must have smelled. After all, practically every domestic servant was on his or her feet all day long, running up and down the stairs carting all manner of goods and supplies—while wearing a heavy wool uniform. One bath a week? The downstairs and the servants' quarters must not have smelled like roses!

BUTLER'S TIP

A household employs domestic staff for three main reasons:

1. *To clean the toilets.*

2. *To make the beds.*

3. *To serve dinner on time.*

If you work in the service industry, these are your *raisons d'être.*

THE HISTORY OF CALLING BELLS

SOME OF YOU MAY REMEMBER the stunning country residence at Dyrham Park in Britain, used as the location for the wonderful film *Remains of the Day*. In real life, the household inventory log of Dyrham Park, which dates back to 1710, holds the first known reference to calling bells. Before the advent of electricity or the telephone, employers needed a way to communicate with their downstairs staff and to summon them when needed. The calling bells solved that problem. This intricate system comprised a network of tubes that each housed a wire running from the downstairs staff quarters to one room in the upstairs of the residence. When a family member or guest of the house pulled a wire upstairs, a bell would ring downstairs in the staff quarters, summoning the hired help.

Interestingly, when the calling bells were installed at Castle Ward, an 18th-century mansion in Northern Ireland well known for its agriculture and architecture, each bell rang at a different pitch so the staff knew exactly which room was calling and where to go. Calling bells were so popular and effective that by the end of the 18th century they had become a specialty for plumbers and chimney sweeps, who were called on to install and maintain them. Ultimately, speaking tubes replaced calling bells during the mid- to late-19th century, and by the early 20th century, the telephone had become the best method of communication between employers and household staff.

ORDER OF PRECEDENCE

There was a time in history when you sat around a dining table in the "order of precedence." Your seat at the table depended on your station or rank in society, and there were well-established rules about who sat where and why. Today, we may not refer to the order of precedence when preparing for a dinner in our homes, but that doesn't mean we don't apply rules when it comes to seating arrangements.

When I think of the order of precedence, I often recall a memorable moment from the fabulous movie *Gosford Park*. The year is 1932 and the action takes place in a grand English country house. The owner of the house, Sir William McCordle, complains to his wife, Lady Sylvia, about being seated next to Aunt Constance—again. He would much rather sit beside a pretty young lady, or perhaps by his mistress. Lady Sylvia chastises him, saying that he should know better than to ask such a foolish question. After all, they are all aristocrats and therefore the seating arrangement is

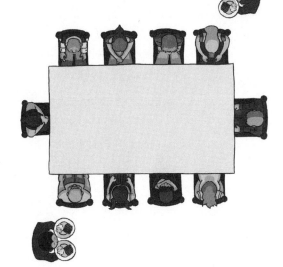

A typical American seating arrangement, with the host and hostess at opposite ends of the table and guests alternating male, female.

always by "order of precedence." I suspect that for Lady Sylvia, the order of precedence served her own purposes!

I think of an order of precedence today as a way of sorting a group of people and finding the most sensible and respectful placement for them around a table. Maybe you're wondering why guests at a table need to be sorted at all. Think about it this way: if you had eighteen people to your home for a formal dinner, you'd have to think about who sat where or chaos would ensue. And if you have ever organized a wedding banquet, you know all too well how important it is to think about seating, because you want your guests to feel comfortable and at ease with those around them. An order of precedence ensures that nobody is offended by something as trivial as their place at the table.

For international state dinners, rank is still one of the factors that determine seating at the table. Other factors could include the relationship of guests to the hosts and any national or regional customs. American tables are typically organized so that guests alternate male and female, with the host at one end of the table and the hostess at the other. Ideally, the host will have the highest-ranking female guest on his right and the second-highest-ranking female to his left. And the hostess will have the highest-ranking male guest to her right and the second-highest-ranking male to her left. The order of precedence will follow in this way down the table.

To the right, you'll find abridged lists of rank often used in Canada and the United States to determine seating at a formal table.

BUTLER'S TIP

Titles rather than surnames are used when speaking to an official. For example, you would say "Mr. Prime Minister" and not "Prime Minister MacDonald" when speaking to the prime minister of Canada.

CANADIAN ORDER OF PRECEDENCE

The Queen

Governor General of Canada

Prime Minister of Canada

Chief Justice of Canada

Speaker of the Senate

Speaker of the House of Commons

Ambassadors, High Commissioners, Ministers Plenipotentiary

Canadian Cabinet Ministers and Secretaries of State

Leader of the Opposition

Members of the Queen's Privy Council for Canada

Premiers of each Province

Commissioners and Leaders of the Northwest Territories,
    Yukon and Nunavut

AMERICAN UNOFFICIAL ORDER OF PRECEDENCE

The order of precedence is followed closely in the United States at all times. Note that in North America, spouses are generally extended the same courtesy as the ranked spouse. With that being said, the art of a perfect seating arrangement is understanding the purpose of a particular event, and seating guests accordingly. Below is a partial list of the American order of precedence.

President

Vice President

Speaker of the House of Representatives

Chief Justice

Former Presidents

BUTLER'S TIP

In Canada, the order of precedence dictates that premiers be seated according to when their province joined Confederation. The longer the province has been in Canada, the better the seat at the table.

Secretary of State

Secretary General of the United Nations

Ambassadors of Foreign Powers

Widows of Former Presidents

Ministers of Foreign Powers (Chiefs of Diplomatic Missions)

Associate Justices of the Supreme Court

The Cabinet (Secretaries and Attorneys)

Director, Office of Management and Budget

The United States Representative to the United Nations

Members of the Senate

Governors of States

Former Vice Presidents

Members of the House of Representatives

OFFICIAL STATE RECEPTION PROTOCOL

Not many of us will ever attend an official state reception, but much of the etiquette around such events applies equally to other important functions. Here are some tips:

• *Be on time:* When it comes to important events, there is no such thing as "fashionably late." Be a few minutes early if you will have to check your coat or if you don't know exactly where to go.

• *Do not lobby:* An official event is not the time to lobby for your cause, no matter what cause it is. Use the event as a social time to get to know people, and contact your new connections on specific matters after the event is over.

- *Never ask for more food:* Asking for a second helping of something will draw unwanted attention. Large events are generally planned down to the minute. By asking for more food you may upset the timing of a dinner, and insult your host or hostess.

- *Connect with your host and hostess:* Make an effort to speak with your host and hostess. Remember to take only a few minutes of their time. If you take too long, an official may politely invite you to enjoy the rest of your evening and point you to the dance floor.

- *Leave gracefully:* Usually, once the guest of honour has left it is your turn to do so. Finish one last dance or cocktail at the bar, then say your good nights and head for the door.

A NOTE ON NOTES

There was a time, long before e-mails, when personal, handwritten correspondence was common. Every proper household had official stationery, and butlers and other heads of staff used this to correspond with tradespeople, as well as for thank-you notes and other household-related correspondence. I love this old-fashioned custom, and I believe that in our fast-paced world, one way of really connecting with someone is to turn back to tradition and offer something personalized—a handwritten thank-you card, a follow-up note or an invitation.

Just as handwritten notes are falling out of fashion, so is fine stationery. Still, I advocate a return to this tradition too. E-mails simply cannot compete with the beauty and elegance of a card or note.

CLARENCE HOUSE

123 Grosvenor Square

London

April 23, 2013

Dear Mrs. Jones,

How very sweet of you to remember my birthday. The flowers you sent arrived early yesterday morning and I put them on my desk so that they would be close by while I worked. The combination of red and yellow is beautiful.

I hope that you and Mr. Jones are well and I promise to call upon you for a visit soon. Again, thank you for your kindness.

Sincerely,
Joanne

THANK-YOU NOTES

Remember these three points when writing a thank-you note:

- Write your note as promptly as possible after attending an event or receiving a gift. Ideally, you should write your note the next day, and no later than a week after.

- When in doubt about who should receive a thank-you note, send one to everyone.

- Be sincere. Even if you don't like a gift, you should express your gratitude for the gesture; find something gracious to say about it.

IRONING A NEWSPAPER

During Victorian and Edwardian times, newsprint was cheap and of poor quality, as was the ink. The printing presses of the time weren't sophisticated enough to get the inks to adhere properly to the paper. The reason the butler ironed the newspaper was so his employers wouldn't get their hands dirty. A dedicated iron was kept downstairs and used only for the newspaper. The paper was delivered directly to the butler each morning and the butler would set to work. In a British household, the newspaper would be laid out by section on a side table or on the breakfast table. If there were several guests, several copies of the paper would be ironed and set out in this way. Believe it or not, there are homes today where the newspaper is still ironed. This is entirely unnecessary (and a tad pretentious, if I do say so myself), but laying out the newspaper in sections is a nice touch even now.

Step 1: Gather an iron, ideally one that is used only for ironing newspapers, some tissue paper and the newspaper.

Step 2: Set the iron on dry (no steam) and on a medium to medium-high setting. Lay one section of the newspaper flat on a clean and dry surface.

Step 3: Place one sheet of tissue on top of the newspaper. Iron from top to bottom and then from left to right. Repeat for each page of the newspaper.

Step 4: Repeat this process with each section of the newspaper. Fold the sections in half.

Step 5: Select an appropriate table or desk in the room to display the newspaper. Lay these out so that each section heading is visible.

PERIODS AND STYLES

It's nice to have a sense of tradition and history. This doesn't mean that we all have to be experts, but we should have a general understanding of periods and styles. For a butler or anyone employed in service, such knowledge is simply part of the trade. A good butler will know the difference between a Queen Anne chair (which has a heart-shaped back) and a Louis-Philippe chair (which has a tall back). How embarrassing to be asked to bring one and return with the other!

This useful list of periods and styles was compiled by Greg Kelley in 2008.

BRITISH REIGNS FROM 1558

Elizabeth I	1558–1603		George III	1760–1820
James I	1603–1625		Regency	1811–1820
Charles I	1625–1649		George IV	1820–1830
Commonwealth	1649–1660		William IV	1830–1837
Charles II	1660–1685		Victoria	1837–1901
James II	1685–1688		Edward VII	1901–1910
William & Mary	1689–1702		George V	1910–1936
Anne	1702–1714		Edward VIII	1936
George I	1714–1727		George VI	1936–1952
George II	1727–1760		Elizabeth II	1952–

GUIDE TO BRITISH STYLES AND PERIODS

Gothic	16th century and earlier
Baroque	Circa 1620–1700
Puritan	Mid 17th century
Rococo with Chinoiserie & Gothic	Circa 1730–1760
Neo-classical	Circa 1760–1800
Empire	Circa 1800–1815
Regency	Circa 1800–1830
Victorian eclecticism including revivals of Rococo, Gothic, Japonaiserie	Circa 1830–1900
Arts and Crafts & Aesthetic Movement	Circa 1880–1900
Art Nouveau and Liberty	Circa 1890–1920
Art Deco	Circa 1920–1940
Modern Movement	From circa 1940

FRENCH REIGNS AND PERIODS

Louis XIII	1610–1643	Restoration	1815–1830
Louis XIV	1643–1715	Louis XVIII	1814–1824
Regence	1715–1723	Charles X	1824–1830
Louis XV	1723–1774	Louis-Philippe	1830–1848
Louis XVI	1774–1793	Second Empire	1848–1870
Directoire	1793–1799	Third Republic	1871–1940
Empire	1799–1815		

PRINCIPAL JAPANESE PERIODS

Heian period	794–1185
Kamakura period	1185–1336
Muromachi period	1336–1573
Momoyama period	1573–1615
Edo period	1615–1868
Meiji period	1868–1912

PRINCIPAL CHINESE DYNASTIES

Shang	16th century–11th century		The Five Dynasties	907–960
Western Zhou	11th century–770 BC		Liao	916–1125
Eastern Zhou	770–256 BC		Northern Song	960–1127
Warring States	453–221 BC		Jin	1115–1234
Quin	221–206 BC		Southern Song	1127–1279
Han	206 BC–AD 220		Yuan	1279–1368
The Six Dynasties	220–580		Ming	1368–1644
Sui	581–618		Qing	1644–1916
Tang	618–907			

REIGNS DURING MING AND QUING DYNASTIES

Ming			*Quing*	
Hongwu	1368–1398		Shunzhi	1644–1661
Yongle	1403–1424		Kangxi	1662–1722
Xuande	1426–1435		Yongzheng	1723–1735
Chenghua	1465–1487		Qianlong	1736–1795
Hongzhi	1488–1505		Jiaqing	1796–1820
Zhengde	1506–1521		Daoguang	1821–1850
Jiajing	1522–1566		Xianfeng	1851–1861
Longqing	1567–1572		Tongzchi	1862–1874
Wanli	1573–1619		Guangxu	1875–1908
Tianqi	1621–1627		Zuantong	1909–1912
Chongzhen	1628–1644		Hongxian	1916–

GEORGE WASHINGTON'S RULES OF CIVILITY AND DECENT BEHAVIOUR

At the age of sixteen, young George Washington was instructed by his schoolmaster to copy out by hand the 110 "Rules of Civility and Decent Behaviour in Company and Conversation." This work, originally created by French Jesuits in 1595, was a list of rules for proper social conduct and good manners. It is presumed that this was part of a school exercise in penmanship, but "Washington's Rules" became very much a part of this great man's life and an important legacy in the field of etiquette. Here are my top twelve favourites:

	George Washington's Rules	Modern-Day Translation
1.	Every action done in Company, ought to be with some sign of respect, to those that are present.	Treat everyone with respect.
2.	When in Company, put not your hands to any part of the body not usually discovered. Put not off your cloths in the presence of others, nor go out your chamber half dressed.	Use your hands in a dignified way. Do not parade around in a state of undress. Generally, do not embarrass others.
3.	Kill no vermin as fleas, lice ticks, et cetera in the sight of others. If you see any filth or thick spittle, put your foot dexterously upon it. If it be upon the cloths of your companions, put it off privately, and if it be upon your own cloths, return thanks to him who puts it off.	If there's a "fly in your soup" or elsewhere, try not to make a fuss but instead get rid of the thing as discreetly as possible.
4.	Keep your nails clean and short, also your hands and teeth clean yet without showing any great concern for them.	Keep your hands clean and well manicured, and maintain good oral hygiene, but don't show either off too much.
5.	In writing or speaking, give to every person his due title according to his degree and the custom of the place.	Address others with respect and tact. (For instance, treat a judge with respect within his or her courtroom.)
6.	Let thy ceremonies in courtesy be proper to the dignity of his place with whom thou converses for it is absurd to act the same with a clown and a prince.	Employ decorum that is appropriate to your current situation. You wouldn't behave the same way towards a queen and a flower merchant. Use proper ceremonies depending on the environment and company.
7.	Wherein you reprove another be unblameable yourself; for example is more prevalent than precepts.	If you criticize someone else of something, make sure you are not guilty of it yourself. As the expression goes, "People in glass houses shouldn't throw stones."
8.	In your apparel be modest and endeavor to accommodate nature, rather than to procure admiration.	Dress modestly and comfortably, and not to gain attention from others.
9.	Associate yourself with men of good quality if you esteem your own reputation; for 'tis better to be alone than in bad company.	Associate with good people. It is better to be alone than in bad company.
10.	Be not apt to relate news if you know not the truth thereof. In discoursing of things you have heard, name not your author.	Do not be quick to talk about something when you don't have all the facts.
11.	Undertake not what you cannot perform, but be careful to keep your promise.	Do not start what you cannot finish. Keep your promises.
12.	Labour to keep alive in your breast that little spark of celestial fire called conscience.	Don't allow yourself to become jaded by your environment and neglect your conscience.

Part Two

The Butler Speaks

WHAT IS A BUTLER? And given that butlers are relatively uncommon today, why care about their roles? My firm belief is that even if butlers are no longer standard in most stately homes, we might all benefit in our everyday lives by learning the skills and emulating the qualities that made them indispensable to their employers. Keep in mind that a butler can be male or female. While it's true that traditionally men have performed the role, today there are women who do a wonderful job of butlering.

I believe a good butler should exhibit the following characteristics:

- A desire to serve
- Discretion
- Interest
- Ability to anticipate
- Curiosity

It may surprise you that these skills aren't practical in

nature. Let me explain. What do I mean when I say a butler has *a desire to serve*? To me, a true butler is someone who makes others feel completely at ease, and that means seeing to their needs before his or her own. A butler has a strong desire to be of service to others and he never ceases to learn. Service to others is rewarding and generous, and there's much to be learned from the butler by adopting a spirit of generosity and selflessness with anyone in your life.

Discretion separates a good butler from a great one. A great butler has the ability to go about his or her work almost invisibly. In fact, invisibility is a trait that to this day continues to be much sought after in the service industry. Invisibility is something many employers pay dearly for! My dear friend and fellow butler Mr. John Robertson has been in the business for more than twenty-five years, and has worked at and trained butlers for major hotels in London, private families, yacht staff and more. I love hearing Mr. Robertson talk about the trade. One of things he believes identifies the extraordinary butler is his ability to enter a room and be *less* in the room than before he entered. This paradox typifies something I try to teach everyone I train in butlering—that the very best butlers blend into the environment so much that they become part of it, allowing occupants of the room a sense of privacy and security even when they are not alone.

There's a perfect example of a butler's discretion in the movie *Remains of the Day*, starring Sir Anthony Hopkins in the role of the butler, Mr. Stevens. Near the end of the movie, Christopher Reeve as estate owner Jack Lewis asks Mr. Stevens his opinion about a conversation he must have overheard as he was in the room when it happened. Mr. Stevens responds to Lewis as though he hadn't heard a thing and has no memory of the conversation at all. He is the consummate butler, behaving with perfect discretion (and indirectly assuring his employer that he is not a gossip).

Another key skill of the butler, and one that differentiates the mediocre from the great, involves understanding the difference between being *interested* and *interesting*. They are not the same! In the hospitality industry, waiters are often instructed to be "interesting"—to become part of the atmosphere of the restaurant and to entertain diners between courses. The wait staff may even be one of the reasons why patrons return to a particular restaurant. The opposite is required of a butler in a professional household. The butler must be interested in understanding his employer's needs and requirements, but he is never on show or expected to be the focal point of attention. He should, at all times, maintain a calm and demure demeanour. He should always allow his employer to be the centre of attention.

Imagine that you are a butler in a fine household, and you've just thrown a marvellous party that went off without a hitch. Every guest in attendance realizes full well that, as the butler, you and your staff handled the party details—the invitations, the food, the drink, the decor, et cetera. As the guests are leaving, one of the guests approaches you rather than the hosts and pays you a lovely compliment on the floral arrangements in the reception hall. A truly refined butler would not say thank you in return because that would be accepting the compliment personally. Instead, he or she would say, "Thank you very much for this compliment. I'll be sure to tell your hosts how much you loved the flowers." After paying the compliment forward to his employers, the butler would then pass the message along to them.

Another skill that clearly defines the butler is the *ability to anticipate*. When I am asked to recommend butlers to employers, I often get this question: "Charles, where can I find someone who can anticipate my needs?" If I were smart enough to know how to teach the skill of anticipation, I would be busy filling butler orders around the world! Alas, this skill is not easily taught. It's innate or it's not. But I must tell you that the ability to anticipate your employer's needs—whether you are a butler or not—is a powerful one that trumps almost any other.

As I travel around the world working in hotels and private residences or giving seminars on household management, I often speak about something I learned from my stepfather: *curiosity*. No matter what your profession, curiosity allows your mind to be open to learning new things. This ultimately makes you a more dynamic and attractive person to everyone you meet, including your employers. Whether you are a butler, a stockbroker or a taxi driver, nurture your curiosity. The knowledge and skills you seek by being curious will make you a better professional and a better human being.

The professional butler should not be the centre of attention, but many, even today, are in the privileged position of both watching history unfold and orchestrating events behind the scenes. Being on the sidelines and watching ceremonial dinners take place and important decisions being made around a dinner table can be exciting. Though a butler will never tell, he may watch the evening news at the end of the day and think to himself with pride, *I was part of the team that allowed that moment to happen.* For me, this feeling is my private reward and something of which I am deeply proud.

TYPES OF BUTLERS

Ever since the first butlers began taking care of wine (which was originally the butler's primary duty), there has been an incredible evolution in the butler's role. Today, there are many different kinds of butlers, and each performs slightly different duties.

TRADITIONAL ENGLISH BUTLER

Upstairs Downstairs, the British television show from the 1970s, was meticulously researched and produced. It introduced viewers to Mr. Hudson, the quintessential English butler. This position survives today in large, formal households, whether these are private residences of established, inherited wealth or newer residences, such as ambassadors' homes, that want to keep the traditions of service alive.

His day (for women were seldom seen in this role historically) revolves primarily around preparing and presenting three meals a day in the dining room, but also includes the setting and service of additional food and drinks for the family and guests—everything from daily family dinners to simple supper trays to weekly dinner parties or grand entertainments. The butler is also responsible for the service of afternoon tea (a fixture in established English houses). It is the butler who makes the sandwiches as well as the tea, as the chef or cook is occupied with dinner preparations. The butler is responsible for all china, silver and stemware and, with the housekeeper's assistance, for the table linens. He maintains the wine cellar and is knowledgeable about wine selection and service. He is also responsible for the male staff in the house—hiring, training and discipline. If no footman or junior butler is employed, the butler answers the front door in the evenings, or during a formal occasion. The butler, along with the governess, takes care of front-door reception and is allowed to come and go through the front door, while all other staff and tradespeople use the trades entrance. It is not unusual for the butler to assume a dual role as valet to the gentleman of the house. For the most part, the butler functions as the single point of contact between the employers and all other staff.

MODERN HOUSEHOLD BUTLER

As the name suggests, this person works in a private household. Today these butlers are not only in service but act as executive managers, taking care of everything from other household employees to budgets, banking, travel arrangements and any or all personal issues as required by the employer. Over time this butler develops a personal relationship with his or her employer. The job is generally well paid. Household butlers can be live-in or live-out. They may be the only household staff within a residence or they may run very large homes and be responsible for other staff. If there is a household manager, then the butler traditionally reports to him or her.

HOTEL BUTLER

Within the past fifteen years, this new type of butler has become popular as top hotels around the world become more competitive and high-end clients expect sophisticated service. The hotel butler is the only point of contact for the guest and will communicate the guest's requests to the relevant departments within the hotel. The butler would, for example, call Room Service on the guest's behalf and serve the meal in the suite. Or if the guest leaves for a mid-morning walk, the butler would call Housekeeping to have someone refresh the suite. This is a challenging position because the butler is not familiar with the guest's lifestyle, so may find it difficult to anticipate his or her needs. This position is not well paid, but the job can be lucrative with good gratuities.

CORPORATE BUTLER

I remember hearing about corporate butlers for the first time in the early 1980s; however, I am sure this job existed much earlier. A corporate butler is someone who works within the executive office of a large company. The corporate butler is responsible for dealing with all the food and beverage requirements of the executive office. This job is well paid, but the real reason why people like this position is that they like the steady Monday to Friday hours, plus holidays off. Also, they generally are entitled to the same corporate benefits as other employees.

PROPERTY MANAGEMENT BUTLER

This is the newest type of butler. It was introduced in Asia (and primarily China) in the late 1980s and early 1990s. This type of butler really does not have the traditional duties we know in the West. He generally works in large upscale apartment buildings, interacting with tenants and apartment owners on behalf of the apartment superintendants or property managers. He schedules all apartment repairs, and deals with special requests, like a major renovation.

THE LANGUAGE OF THE BUTLER

No matter how many times you may have heard this, I believe it bears repeating: "You have just one chance to make a first impression." When you see someone for the first time—a future employer, a blind date or an anchor presenting the news—you immediately form an impression of that person, be it positive or negative or neutral. This impression is made within seconds of two individuals meeting and is extremely difficult to change. Fair or not, that first feeling is based on countless tangibles and intangibles, including physical appearance, body language and attitude.

Imagine you are one of two people applying for a job. As the first candidate interviewed, you stand tall, you have a firm handshake, you look the interviewer in the eye, you smile confidently. The second candidate, however, has a slumped posture, pulls away her hand too fast during a handshake and looks at the ground when others speak. Even before either candidate has said a word, an impression has been made. As candidate 1, you've set the right tone, whereas candidate 2 is already sending the message that he or she can't handle the job.

A good butler has much to teach us about how to make a good first impression. He knows that body language is an important, non-verbal part of communication, as are gestures, poses, movements and expressions. As he stands by the door, answers the phone or even goes about his daily chores, his voice, posture and demeanour exemplify calm dignity. Think of this as a recipe for first-impression success, no matter what the circumstance.

Here are a few pointers every butler knows will help to create a good first impression.

- When meeting someone for the first time, repeat his or her name in your conversation. A butler will call the guest Mr. or Mrs., plus their last name. He will never address a guest by first name.

- Use the appropriate amount of formality depending on the circumstance, but whenever you're uncertain, err on the side of being more formal, at least at first. Most people will tell you if they'd prefer a less formal style of address, but few will tell you when you've erred and gone too informal.

- Listen carefully when you meet someone, not only to the words a person uses but also to their underlying meaning. Respond when appropriate, and be generous and gracious.

- Always maintain eye contact.

- Be careful of using humour. If you are meeting someone for the first time, you do not want to offend them.

- Check your ego at the door. Wait until you have established credibility before you even consider challenging someone you've just met.

- Choose your words carefully because, rightly or wrongly, what you say will be used to judge your intelligence, education, culture and abilities.

HOW SHOULD A BUTLER STAND?

A butler's appearance and demeanour is important at all times. His or her conduct, work and stance will be viewed and judged by employers and fellow employees. In fact, posture and stance are important to any professional, and you will always look more polished and poised if you stand up straight. The person who is slumped over is considered sloppy, while the person who stands tall, hands behind back, is considered attentive and professional.

WHERE TO PLACE THE HANDS

When standing correctly at the front door, in the dining room or at any point within service, your hands should always be behind you, clasped together while you stand in a tall position. This keeps the front of your suit pulled back, clean, neat and wrinkle free.

DO

Standing with your hands in front of you is considered rude. Also, for a gentleman, it's seen as unhygienic.

HOW TO BOW CORRECTLY

There are two methods of bowing: the first is from the head and the second is from the waist. Both are appropriate when done correctly, but it is important to know the difference and when to use each method.

BOWING FROM THE HEAD

This is the correct way for a butler to bow when acknowledging his or her employers and their guests. Keep your arms by your side. This is subtle and understated.

BOWING FROM THE WAIST

Do not bow from the waist in household service. It is a more formal gesture than bowing from the neck and is performed as a traditional greeting, or in some Asian cultures as an expression of thanks or apology. The deeper and longer the bow, the more formal the gesture.

HOW TO CURTSY CORRECTLY

It is protocol in European cultures for women to curtsy when they greet royalty.

1. Stand upright with your right foot behind your left heel.

2. As you bend your knees slightly, bow your head a little, then return to the standing position a moment later.

GREETING EXPECTED GUESTS AT THE FRONT DOOR

When answering the door, maintain an upright posture, be polite and greet guests with a warm smile. Help them with any coats, winter boots, umbrellas, et cetera, and know what you're going to do with these. There is nothing worse than meeting a guest on a blustery winter day and saying, "Oh dear. I have no idea where to put your coat and boots."

GREETING UNEXPECTED GUESTS AT THE FRONT DOOR

When I was a child, my father used to drag me around to visit friends he hadn't thought to call ahead of time. The two of us just showed up out of nowhere and I sometimes sensed that we were not welcome or, more to the point, that we were intruding at the wrong moment. I must admit, it wasn't until I was in my first apartment that I realized how much I dislike unannounced visitors. I found it disruptive and rude to have people drop by out of the blue.

So what do you do when someone arrives unexpectedly? Well, two wrongs don't make a right, so first, be polite, greet the guests and say how happy you are to see them. But remember: it is okay to say politely, "It's so nice to see you, but I'm sorry, this is not a good time." Don't feel obligated to receive guests when it is not convenient. Here are some gracious things you might say to well-meaning but unannounced visitors:

- *"Thank you for stopping by. It means a lot to me, but I'm in the middle of something personal. Can we get together later this week?"*

- *"I'm so glad to see you, but I am just about to go out the door. Let's call each other over the next few days and do that dinner and movie we've been talking about."*

- *"I'm so glad you came by, but to be honest I'm not feeling well today. My plan is to spend the day in bed reading and resting. I hope you don't mind that I call you next week and we can set something up?"*

THE ETIQUETTE OF DOORS AND DOORWAYS

In times gone by, it was customary for men to open doors for women, whether at the front entrance of a private home, at a restaurant or at a shop. This was as true for strangers as it was for family. The husband, for instance, would open the door for his wife if they were both entering an establishment together; similarly, if a man arrived at a shop at the same time as a woman he didn't know, he would open the door for her to let her pass through first.

Today, in public settings as well as in private ones, you'll see a lot of doors slamming in people's faces—male and female! In my opinion, it is rude for a man or woman to not take a few seconds to hold a door for someone.

HOW TO OPEN A DOOR FOR A STRANGER

Whether you are male or female, it's polite to open a door for someone if you are both entering an establishment at the same time. So, how do you do this without it being awkward? If you are approaching a door at exactly the same time as someone else, avoid running ahead to get to the door first. Instead, keep your pace even, and when you arrive at the door, simply say, "I've got it," and reach for the door handle. As you open the door, step aside and hold the door wide. This allows the other person to pass through easily. If you don't step aside, the person stepping through has to step around you first, and most doorways are built for one, not two! A polite person will always say "Thank you" to the person who holds the door open, and you may respond with "You're welcome." Once the person has passed the threshold, you may follow.

HOW TO OPEN A DOOR FOR A COMPANION

This happens all the time: you are walking side by side with a business colleague or friend and you arrive at a closed door. Who should open it and how should this be done without one person crossing awkwardly in front of the other and interrupting the natural flow of conversation? I lean towards the traditional rule where a man and woman are involved, which calls for the man to open the door. But regardless of who opens it, there's a correct way. The person closest to the door who can use his or her right hand to open it should be the one to move forward first. This avoids the "awkward cross." The one exception is if your companion requires assistance (such as an elderly person, or someone with luggage), in which case it is polite to excuse yourself for walking in front of your companion, open the door and allow him or her to pass through.

HOW TO CARRY TRAYS

CARRYING TRAYS WITH HANDLES
When carrying a tray with handles, remember to use the handles. Sometimes, negotiating through closed doors and staircases can be a challenge, but using both hands to support the tray will give you better stability and balance.

CARRYING TRAYS WITHOUT HANDLES
Holding a tray without handles can become second nature with a bit of practice.

Carry a tray without handles by resting it on the flat portion of one hand.

DO

When walking with the tray, keep your second hand behind your back. Use that hand to open or close doors.

DON'T

Never carry a tray on your fingertips. This makes the tray unstable (and looks pretentious).

DON'T

Never carry by the rim.

SERVING A TRAY IN BED

There is a right and a wrong way to serve a breakfast tray in bed. The etiquette depends on whether it's a man or woman in bed and who is serving.

DON'T

It is incorrect for a gentleman to face the lady while serving her a tray in bed. Most likely, she will be wearing a low-cut dressing gown and this may make her feel self-conscious. Similarly, a female butler serving a male gentleman should avoid facing him.

DO

When serving a lady in bed, stand beside the bed facing forward. This is more discreet and respectful.

DO

When serving someone of the same sex, face the person being served, allowing for direct eye contact.

THE BUTLER'S TOOLKIT: THE BUTLER'S TRAY

A traditional butler's tray was originally designed for serving beverages and food. It was a folding table that he could carry anywhere, whether serving drinks in the drawing room, lunch on the patio or coffee in the library. The butler's tray is an indispensable tool and every household should have one.

There are several types of butler's tray. Some have a slight rim for carrying beverages or plates; others have specific functions, such as a cutlery tray for setting the table.

PUSHING IN A GUEST'S CHAIR AT THE TABLE

Even in social settings today, it's gentlemanly when dining to help a lady with her chair. This applies not only to a butler but to any dinner guest in a restaurant. Remember that while this is a lovely touch in a restaurant, it's not at all appropriate for a business setting. Believe me when I say that the female CEO is not going to be impressed by the male underling who tries to help her into her chair in the boardroom. As with all etiquette, there is a right time and place.

With both hands on the back of the chair and your foot on the foot of the chair, push the chair forward until the seat touches the back of the guest's knees. The guest will automatically bend her knees and sit. You will need the strength of your hands and foot to move the chair to the table once the guest is seated.

DO

DON'T

DON'T

Do not push in the chair with your knee as this may damage the chair (or your knee!). Also, you will not get enough force behind you to move the chair forward.

Do not push in the chair from the top only. This will tip the chair forward. The force of your push needs to come from both the top and bottom of the chair as detailed in the first illustration above.

MAKING INTRODUCTIONS

Making introductions correctly is crucial, and this has nothing to do with old-fashioned manners and everything to do with making potentially awkward or uncomfortable situations simple and stress-free. Introductions used to be much more formal than they are now. Over time, the rules have relaxed. Now, most introductions go as follows: "Harry, this is my friend Sally." My belief is that this relaxed way of introducing people has become the norm simply because we don't know what else to do.

There are situations where this kind of informal introduction isn't appropriate, and a few simple guidelines can help everyone involved feel more at ease. Here's how to become the master of the introduction.

1. Introduce the person of lesser status to the person of higher status. Status may be based on rank, order of precedence, age or gender. Here are some examples:

- In a business setting, the junior employee is introduced to the senior employee, regardless of gender or age.
- In most circumstances, the younger person is introduced to the older person.
- In social situations, the man is generally introduced to the woman (regardless of status).

2. For introductions involving multiple people, mention the name of the most important person first.

3. When introducing dignitaries or other distinguished people, use the word "present" instead of the word "introduce," as in, "Your Grace, may I present Mr. MacPherson."

4. Introduce people formally in the following way: "May I introduce to you Mr. MacPherson from Canada."

5. Dorothea Johnson, founder of the prestigious Protocol School of Washington, advises that when making introductions, one should never say, "John, may I present you to Carol." The correct phrasing is, "present to you." She offers a clever way for us to remember the difference. Think of the rock band U2. Rock bands aren't known for their etiquette, so this order is incorrect. "To you," unlike the band name, will always be correct!

6. Correctly pronounce names and titles.

7. Make eye contact.

8. Smile and speak in a warm and friendly voice.

9. Speak clearly.

Making introductions can be intimidating. If you're unsure of etiquette, practise at home, over and over again, until you know the basics. You want the correct words to roll off your tongue. Proper introductions are probably not something you'll ever be complimented for, even if people do admire your grace and style. But if you get an introduction wrong, believe me, people *will* notice . . .

THE DO'S AND DON'TS OF A HANDSHAKE

The handshake is a key point of etiquette because it's an important aspect of making a first impression. A badly executed handshake, poorly timed, will inevitably create a negative impression. You have probably experienced a handshake by a "bone crusher." This happens when a handshake is performed with such force that it actually hurts. This kind of greeting does not show dominance, as some people believe;

rather, it makes the person executing the handshake look like a callous idiot. The footballer who is introduced to a ballerina and who uses a "bone crusher" handshake is not endearing himself to the dancer. Quite the opposite, in fact.

So, what makes a handshake effective? It should be genuine and friendly; it should *not* be tentative or indifferent. The palm should be warm and dry, not cold and clammy. If you do have clammy hands, keep them out of your pockets so that air circulates, and carry a small handkerchief in your right hand that you can subtly pass to your left hand behind your back before you shake. Remember: your grip should be firm and strong (but not bone-crushing!); it should not be limp and lifeless. Balance is the key to a good handshake.

THINGS TO REMEMBER WHEN SHAKING HANDS
- Maintain eye contact. (This is a Western approach. Remember that in the Asian part of the world, eye contact is often considered disrespectful, so don't be offended by this cultural difference, and adapt your approach to the context.)
- Smile warmly.
- Focus your attention on the person to whom you're being introduced or who is being introduced to you.
- Listen to what the person in front of you is saying.
- Keep your hand open and connect "web to web" (palm to palm).
- Gauge the duration of the handshake by paying close attention to the other person. A good rule of

thumb is to pump your hand three times or for about three seconds.

WHEN TO SHAKE SOMEONE'S HAND

It's important to know when to shake someone's hand—as well as when not to. A good rule of thumb is to offer a handshake "more often than not." In business, this includes the following situations:

- Meeting co-workers for the first time—both upon greeting and saying goodbye.
- Being introduced to new business contacts.
- Congratulating someone.

DO NOT OFFER A HANDSHAKE WHEN:

- The person you wish to greet is of a higher rank or position. Wait for this individual to offer his or her hand first.
- Beginning an interview. Follow the lead of the interviewer.
- The other person has their hands full.

Because of fears over the transmission of viruses, there are times, for example during a bad flu season, when people may feel particularly uncomfortable shaking hands. In fact it may have people running for the hand sanitizer. (If you're the one concerned about the spread of germs, remember to run for the hand sanitizer discreetly.)

HOW TO OFFER YOUR BUSINESS CARD

The etiquette for handing out a business card is just as important as that for shaking someone's hand. While business card etiquette is much more relaxed in Western cultures, it is still important to be respectful in how you approach this exchange.

The more formal Asian method of offering a business card with two hands is becoming more common around the world. What I find interesting is that when you use this method in the West, people are impressed. It makes you appear both worldly and knowledgeable to use the formal style. Follow the protocol below and you will never go wrong.

DO

Always present and receive a business card using both hands. In some cultures, the business card is considered a representation of the owner and therefore should be treated with respect. Make a point of reviewing the card and commenting on it before putting it away.

DON'T

Do not give your business card using just one hand. This is considered arrogant and suggests that the information on your card is unimportant.

Do not give out your business card holding the bottom of the card. This is awkward for the person who receives it.

DON'T

CARS

CAR ETIQUETTE

As a butler, your interaction with your guests begins at the moment of arrival and concludes after the guest's departure. If you are a guest at a hotel that has butler service or a car valet, or if you are lucky enough to be invited to a fine home with such service, you should know a few things about how front-door greeting works.

As your car drives up, the butler or car valet will approach the car. He or she may not immediately open the car door. Instead, the good butler or car valet will discreetly look into the car (if the windows aren't tinted) to see if you are ready to get out. For your part, remember that you don't have to rush. If you are on the phone, finish your call before you step out. Take the time to gather your belongings and collect yourself. If the butler or car valet opens the door before you are ready to emerge, simply let him or her know that you need a moment. Your car door will be closed again and only opened when you signal that you wish to step out.

When you are departing a fine house or hotel, the butler or car valet will try to anticipate your needs by having the car ready with chilled bottled water, a newspaper and other appropriate amenities. Don't be shy. If there's something you need, ask for it. A good butler will always help you into the car and then signal to the driver that you are ready to depart. You can tell the experienced from the inexperienced butler or valet by the way they signal the driver. A knock on the hood of the car rather than a tap on the window is considered a bit rude because the sound travels inside to the passenger.

In a social situation, it's a nice touch for a man to open the car door for a woman; however, in a business setting, it's best to let a woman open her own door. Either way, if the woman is wearing a skirt, it's a polite gesture for the man to offer to slide into the back seat first. Why? If you don't know, that's because you've never tried to slide across a back seat while wearing a skirt! Any woman will tell you that it's a challenge to do this gracefully, and a gentleman who quietly says, "Perhaps it's easiest if I get in first?" is saving the woman from awkwardness.

PASSENGER ETIQUETTE

If you are a guest in someone's car, be respectful. Don't change the radio station, adjust the heat setting or, heaven forbid, light up a cigarette. If you are uncomfortable with the temperature, politely ask the driver to change it. You can adjust the seat if necessary, though. Also, if you are driving a guest in your car, remember that there's nothing worse than feeling unsafe in someone else's vehicle. Drive cautiously and alertly. If for any reason you need to slam on the brakes or swerve to avoid a collision, apologize to your passenger. Avoid the temptation to insult, swear or complain about other drivers—unless, that is, you're on a mission to never drive these guests anywhere again!

Step 1: Stand by the car door to receive the guest. When the passenger is ready to disembark, open the door. If the passenger is a woman, offer your hand or wrist as needed. If the passenger is a man, hold the car door firmly as he exits. Never lean into the car. Many people find this an intrusion into their personal space.

Step 2: Give the guest your full attention from the moment you open the door. Greet the guest by name, if possible, and then observe his/her body language to determine the appropriate level of interaction.

BUILDING THE PERFECT FIRE

Fires in the drawing rooms of yesteryear served a more practical purpose than they do today—warmth. But now, fires in the hearth provide comfort, ambience and even entertainment. Building the perfect fire starts with good dry wood. Ideally, wood is cured for one year to allow all the moisture to escape before it is lit.

There are two things you must remember when using a fireplace. First, before you light the fire, make sure the damper is open. Second, once the fire is burning, cover the hearth opening with the fireplace screen or metal curtain to prevent sparks from flying out into the room.

Step 1: To protect the fireplace from excessive heat, make sure that there are a few ashes remaining from the previous fire. Check to make sure the damper is open. Crumple single sheets of newspaper and place loosely under the grate.

Step 2: Place pieces of kindling on top of the grate. There should be spaces between the kindling for air circulation.

Step 3: On top of the kindling, place two dry logs side by side, leaving some space in between.

Step 4: Place two more logs across the top of the first pair. Again, the logs should be evenly stacked to maintain the space in the middle of the woodpile for air circulation.

Step 5: This is the perfectly constructed wood stack, with all the components correctly layered, starting with the ashes, newspaper, kindling and dry wood. Air will circulate up and through the logs. Your fire is now ready to be lit.

THE HISTORY OF THE TELEPHONE
IN THE HOME

ON MARCH 7, 1876, Alexander Graham Bell was granted U.S. patent No. 174,465 for the invention of the telephone. Three days later, on March 10, he made his historic transmission to Mr. Watson and the modern telephone was born. A year later, the first long-distance telephone call took place, and within a short time, the telephone became popular.

At first, the telephone appeared in only the most affluent of Edwardian households, and even then homes usually had just one rather than one in practically every room, the way we have today. The telephone was seen as a "service device," installed either in the butler's pantry or in the staff quarters below stairs and used not for conversation, the way we use it today, but only for the delivery of essential messages.

If you're a fan of *Downton Abbey*, perhaps you recall the funny scene when Mr. Carson, the butler, is dealing with the new phone installed in the servants' quarters downstairs. He is extremely wary of this be-witching device and in the privacy of his room he practises using it. He has no idea how one should answer the telephone, so he tries on various voices and salutations. It is great fun for a modern viewer to watch this moment, because poor Mr. Carson is struggling with something that for us is second nature. I wonder how Mr. Carson would react if he were teleported to the present and offered a cell phone!

AFTERNOON TEA VERSUS HIGH TEA

The ritual of afternoon tea is often credited as the brilliant idea of Anna Maria Stanhope, the Duchess of Bedford. Afternoon tea began in the United Kingdom during the Victorian era and was enjoyed by middle- and upper-class households. Usually served between 3 p.m. and 5 p.m., it was a means of staving off hunger until dinner, which was served later in the evening. Afternoon tea usually consists of a service of tea, with scones, cakes, pastries and/or sandwiches. High tea was a more substantial meal with at least one hot food item served around 6 p.m. and is what we would refer to as the evening meal—dinner. Today, the two kinds of tea are often confused and people frequently use the term "high tea" to refer to an elaborate afternoon tea.

Organizing an afternoon tea is a fantastic way to entertain without fussing too much. If you live in a small apartment, it's much easier to invite family and friends to tea than to dinner, and avoid having to do a lot of cooking. It's also more economical, while at the same time elegant.

TEA SERVICE ELEMENTS

- Beverage: tea service
- Savoury 1: finger sandwiches
- Savoury 2: scones with clotted cream and strawberry jam
- Sweets: miniature cakes and/or pastries

Questions to Answer Before You Start

- How many guests are coming?
- What time will afternoon tea be served?

BUTLER'S TIP

A sign of respect and endearment when hosting an afternoon tea is to ask one of your guests to "play mother," suggesting he or she pour the tea round to the other guests. It's called "playing mother" because the matriarch of the family was the person who traditionally performed this task.

- What kind of tea would each person like to drink?
- Is there a specific selection of sandwiches, scones and cakes required or would an assorted tray of these food items be acceptable?

Once you can answer these questions, you are ready to begin preparations. The table is usually set prior to the arrival of your guests. Serve the tea itself only after your guests arrive (see sample tea tray setup on next page). When you bring in the tea tray, you as the host or hostess may choose to pour the tea into your guests' cups or you may ask one of your guests to pour. The person who pours the tea may add the sugar and milk or lemon for the guests or the guests may serve themselves.

The tea tray should be large enough to hold all the tea service components, excluding the food. The food is usually brought in separately; the food can be served on plates and brought in on a tray or served more traditionally on a tiered cake-stand. If the food is served on a three-tiered stand, it is placed in this order: cakes and pastries on the top tier, scones and clotted cream on the middle tier and tea sandwiches on the bottom tier. You may offer to serve guests or guests may serve themselves.

TABLE COMPONENTS

When afternoon tea is served at a table, lay the table with individual place settings as shown in the illustrations on the next page. Before the tea tray is brought out, ensure the table is set for the correct number of guests. The individual tea table setting will have many of the same elements as an individual place setting.

TEA TABLE SET FOR TWO PEOPLE

Tablecloth (1)

Small Plates (2)

Small Forks (2)

Small Knives (2)

Teacup & Saucer (2)

Teaspoon (2)

Sugar Bowl (1)

Milk Jug (1)

Lemon Slices (2)

Teapot (1)

Hot Water Pot (1)

Flower (1)

Napkins (2)

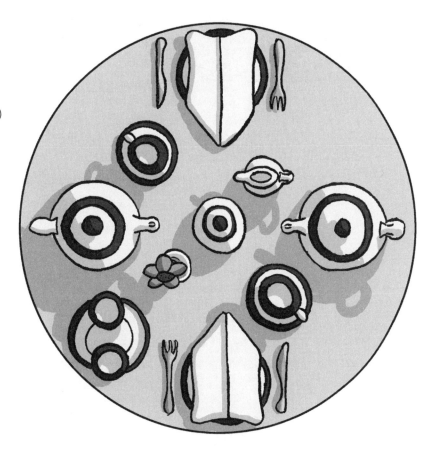

Preparing a tea tray for afternoon tea may seem a straight-forward task, but servers often get it wrong because they have not placed all the necessary components on the tray. There is nothing more frustrating than your employer and his guests waiting for you as you run back to the kitchen or butler's pantry because you forgot something.

Small Plates (2)	Milk Jug (1)
Small Forks (2)	Lemon Slices (2)
Small Knives (2)	Teapot (1)
Teacup & Saucer (2)	Hot Water Pot (1)
Teaspoon (2)	Flower (1)
Sugar Bowl (1)	Napkins (2)

The picture above is the correct full tray setup with all the components you will need to serve a traditional afternoon tea. The tea tray properly set with all the necessary components is placed near the host or hostess and is ready for immediate service.

THE BUTLER'S TOOLKIT: THE BUTLER'S PANTRY

The butler's pantry is his home base, his professional nerve centre. The pantry was where the first telephones in the house were installed, where all the china was found, the silver, and more. It was always located on the ground floor of a house, and all the food would be brought up from the kitchen, plated there and served to the dining room.

HOW TO BREW A POT OF TEA: TEA BAG METHOD

Step 1: Warm the teapot with a little hot water.

Step 2: Swirl the water to heat the teapot.

Step 3: Pour out the hot water through the spout.

Step 4: Add to the teapot one tea bag per cup of water. Make sure that the tea bag tag is hanging out to identify the type of tea.

Step 5: Pour freshly boiled (but not boiling) water over the tea bag.

Step 6: Place the lid back on the teapot and allow the tea to steep 3 to 5 minutes, depending on the type. Then remove the tea bag so that the tea does not become bitter and serve immediately.

HOW TO BREW A POT OF TEA: LOOSE-LEAF METHOD

Step 1: Warm the teapot with a little hot water.

Step 2: Swirl the water to heat the teapot.

Step 3: Pour out the hot water through the spout.

Step 4: Add one teaspoon of loose tea per cup of water, plus one for the teapot.

Step 5: Pour freshly boiled (but not boiling) water over the loose tea.

Step 6: Place the lid back on the teapot to allow the tea to brew 3 to 5 minutes, depending on tea type. Serve immediately after.

COFFEE STYLES AND DESCRIPTIONS

Most people who enjoy coffee are picky about how they take it and even what sort of coffee they drink. Always choose a good, fresh bean, and, if you know how, grind fresh-roasted coffee beans yourself. If that's not possible, opt for good-quality ground coffee, and ask the coffee shop to grind it for you. Coffee beans should always be roasted by professionals because they are very easy to burn. Best to leave it to the experts. There are many styles of coffee and different grinds available. A good host or hostess should be familiar with the various options and be prepared to offer guests a perfectly made cup of coffee.

DEMITASSE   ESPRESSO   CAFÉ AU LAIT   CAPPUCCINO

Demitasse	Freshly brewed, percolated coffee served black without milk or cream in a coffee cup, usually at the end of the meal. Sugar is offered.
Espresso	A concentrated coffee brewed by forcing hot water at high pressure through finely ground coffee. Espresso is served in an espresso cup. Sugar is offered.
Café au lait	Café au lait is made with equal parts strong coffee and hot, steaming milk. Sugar is offered. It is usually served

French style in a bowl, but can also be served in a large cup. The Italian version of café au lait is a caffe latte, consisting of one shot of espresso with a generous amount of steamed milk (a 1:3 ratio). Like café au lait, it is often served in a large bowl or cup, but can also be served in a glass.

Cappuccino   An espresso-based drink consisting of equal parts espresso, steamed milk and frothed milk. It is always served in a cup and can be dusted with either cinnamon or cocoa powder. You should always ask your guests what their preferences are before dusting with cinnamon or cocoa powder. Sugar is offered with cappuccino.

HOW TO GIFT-WRAP A BOX

There's something wonderful about receiving a well-wrapped gift. It makes the recipient feel special, and it shows that the giver cares enough to do things properly. Here are some basic wrapping tips:

- Work on a clean flat surface.
- Remove the price ticket.
- Use sharp scissors to cut the paper so that the edges are clean and straight.
- Use double-sided tape for a seamless look.
- Pull the paper taut and sharply crease all folds.

Step 1: Cut a sheet of paper that will cover the box, adding a 2-inch overlap. Place the box face down in the centre of the paper.

Step 2: Fold over the left side of the paper and secure it with a piece of double-sided tape.

Step 3: Make a small 1/2-inch fold on the edge of the right side of the paper and secure it with double-sided tape. This will create a neat finished edge.

Step 4: Tautly fold over the right side of the paper so that it rests in the centre of the box. Secure it with a piece of double-sided tape.

Step 5: Fold down the ends of the paper to create two side flaps.

Step 6: Crease along the edge of the box as you fold in the side flaps.

Step 7: Crease along the bottom edge as you fold up the bottom flap. The length of this flap should not exceed the top edge of the box.

Step 8: Secure the end with a piece of double-sided tape. Repeat on the other end. Turn the box over for bowing.

TYING THE PERFECT BOW

A beautifully wrapped gift looks even better tied with
a bow. Also, you can use your own style and flair to make
each package you wrap look unique by combining
complementary bows and wrapping paper.

Step 1: Start by measuring the ribbon the entire length of the
package. Make sure you leave excess ribbon extending
towards you.

Step 2: Wrap the ribbon around the length of the box
away from you, keeping the excess end extending
towards you.

Step 3: Taking the piece of ribbon that you wrapped around
the box, cross the ribbon at a 90-degree angle at the
point where the bow will be. Wrap the ribbon under
and around the box and bring the end up on the
other side of the box.

Step 4: Pass the ribbon end over and under the cross point.
Do not tie a knot at this point.

Step 5: Pull the two loose ends tightly to make the ribbon taut.

Step 6: Form the ends of each of the ribbons into equal loops.

Step 7: To make the bow, tie the two loops together just as if you were tying your shoelaces.

Step 8: Now pull the loops tightly, creating a nice bow, and make any final adjustments to make the bow beautiful.

Step 9: Now that you are done, snip the ends of the ribbon on an angle to the desired length.

BUTLER'S TIP

To get a clean cut on the ends of a ribbon, use a sharp pair of scissors.
I suggest you keep a pair of scissors on hand to use only for ribbon.

Part Three

The Etiquette of
Entertaining

ALTHOUGH SOME RULES of conduct existed in even early societies, the etiquette of entertaining over the past three hundred years originated from the elaborate practices of the French royal court of Louis XIV (1638–1715). In his court, rules of social conduct established formality and deference to the royal family. It was important for courtiers and subjects to know court etiquette in order to conduct themselves properly within court circles and higher society. The rules of court etiquette were rigid, and those who were adept at following entertainment etiquette while at court were more likely to advance.

On the other side of the pond, in the United States, George Washington (1732–1799) was also considering etiquette and in particular how to behave in social circumstances. As mentioned earlier, as a youth he copied out 110 "Rules of Civility and Decent Behaviour in Company and Conversation" as a school exercise (some appear on page 38 of this book). These rules greatly influenced President Washington and became a code by which he lived his life.

Since then, many other etiquette mavens have forwarded the cause of good manners. The renowned Mrs. Emily Post (1873–1960) in 1922 wrote the first book of modern-day etiquette; Mrs. Amy Vanderbilt (1908–1974), who called herself "a journalist in the field of etiquette," published the bestselling *Complete Book of Etiquette*; and the legendary Mrs. Letitia Baldrige (1926-2012) wrote over twenty-two books on the subject, and, during her career, successfully brought her tips on etiquette to the White House tables during the Kennedy administration. These authors brought a tradition of elegance to the American public, from those early days all the way to the present.

People may be uncomfortable with entertaining because they simply don't know what to do or how to conduct themselves. I find it helpful to remember the purpose of etiquette: *to show respect to others*. This is true when you're entertaining and when you're a guest in someone's home. Whether it's knowing which fork to use at the lunch table or how to introduce people at a cocktail reception, entertainment etiquette should not be feared but embraced. My goal is to put you at ease so you're not anticipating an event with fear in your heart, wondering, "How am I going to get through this?"

As a former society caterer, I know there are two important rules when entertaining:

1. Make sure everyone has a drink in hand.
2. Make sure everyone has someone to talk to.

Believe it or not, these two tips are more important than the decor, the music or the food being served. At any gathering you host, if you can just make sure people feel comfortable, relaxed and connected with others, your event will be a success.

Another thing to consider, before you entertain, is the shopping. I find the biggest mistake people make is that they wait until the last minute to prepare. If you know you are going to have a party in two weeks, buy things for your bar ahead of time. A professional butler would be dead from exhaustion if he were to try to prepare every aspect of a party on the same day. Whenever I worked as a butler, I planned entertainment events in a series, so instead of spreading out parties over a month, I'd stack them night after night, three in a row. This meant buying flowers only once, shopping once and renting cutlery once. This saved time and energy and made entertaining much more enjoyable for all the household staff involved!

I used to have a small apartment on the Upper West Side of Manhattan. My apartment, like many in Manhattan, had a very small kitchen. Cooking meals for a crowd was a serious challenge, especially given that I had only a tiny bar fridge—and it was in my home office, not in the kitchen! As a former caterer and as a butler, I studied my space and came up with a formula that allowed me to entertain as though I had a big flat on Park Avenue.

My first rule was to never greet guests at my apartment door. When guests would call from downstairs, I would buzz them into the building and meet them in the hallway at the elevator outside my apartment. I would welcome them there and take their coats and any parcels, so that by the time I opened my door and they entered my home, the preliminaries had been taken care of. I also contained the clutter immediately by using my office as a cloakroom. Next, I found a perfect little spot in my living room where I set up a self-serve bar. My second rule was to pour guests their first drink. After that, I invited each guest to help him or herself to the handy, self-serve bar.

When it comes to food, people always have the best of intentions, but unless you can cook throughout the party, complicated menus either fail (nothing ever goes as planned when you're in a rush) or you as the host resent the work because you spend all your time alone in the kitchen. No one wants that—not you and not your guests—so what's the best way to deal with this problem? If you can't hire professional caterers, that's okay. Instead, prepare a buffet menu that is easy both for you and your guests. While working at the famous restaurant Fenton's in Toronto, I learned how to prepare cheese trays that were attractive, interesting and delicious. When I entertained for small or large groups, the cheese board was the centrepiece of my coffee table. I made these ahead of time so that the work was done, and the board included a variety of soft, medium and hard cheeses, from mild to strong. I made two boards in advance, so that when the first one started to look messy and picked over, I could do a quick swap and present a fresh platter.

I would design the entire buffet around one hot item, such as a beef stew or a quiche. The other foods were served at room temperature. This made my job easy because I could lay out the entire table before guests arrived and then spend my time with them, rather than fussing with the food. For lunch or dinner, the additional items on the table would include salads, pâtés, smoked salmon, fresh fruits, cakes, miniature pastries and so on. A typical breakfast buffet at my house would include fresh fruit, pains au chocolate and croissants, cheese and crackers and meringues.

Part of the secret to my entertaining success was that I turned my Canadian antique dining table (which could hold only four or five comfortably) into a buffet table. My apartment living room could then hold ten to twelve people, and everyone would have a place to sit. And all of the food that I served had to be what I call "fork food"—food easily eaten with just a fork and no knife. I would write the menu on a card, so guests would know what had been set out and what was still to come.

When you host any kind of gathering, it is important to watch your guests and ensure that they are having a good time. Do they have a drink in hand? Do they appear to be enjoying the company of those they're talking to or do they need to be rescued? I believe that as a host you can never totally relax. That doesn't mean you can't enjoy your own party, but to make it a success you need to attend to your guests, and this attention is what allows them to relax and have a great time. That said, when an element of your party goes awry (which it often does), don't show your frustration. As the host or hostess, you are the only one who knows exactly what the party was *supposed* to look like; if you share your anxiety with your company, everyone will realize that you've made a mistake.

Also, don't be a snob. If you know certain rules of etiquette but someone in your home does not, it is rude and inappropriate to advise them and make them feel uncomfortable. Always be kind and gracious even when others are not. This is the correct form of behaviour for any host or hostess.

It's possible for a party to succeed too well. I once had a famous supermodel over to my apartment for a party. I was so nervous before she arrived, but my entertainment formula worked well and allowed me to be with her and to enjoy her company instead of being concerned with the food and its presentation (both of which I had taken care of before her arrival). Her mother was in attendance as well, and she loved my easy entertainment style and the atmosphere in my apartment so much that she wanted to buy it!

And finally, whenever I entertain, I like to have bunches of fresh flowers, pleasing background music (at a low volume) and, no matter what, I organize myself so that I have thirty minutes before guests arrive to sit in my living room and relax—ideally with a drink in hand. If you can do all this, I guarantee your party will be a hit!

BUTLER'S TIP

During a party or social gathering, a good butler turns down the telephone ringer on all telephones (except perhaps a kitchen phone or one other in the household). When hosting a party in your home, you may wish to do the same. You will still hear the phone ring, but it won't be disruptive.

TABLE SETTING AND SERVICE

Setting a table can be fun, and whenever possible I like to do
it ahead of time, even for simple functions, so that I don't tire
myself out just before my guests arrive. When it comes to
"tabletop design," as the "fancy people" like to call setting a
table, the fashion is simple and elegant. No matter what kind of
home you have, you want a table to be inviting for your guests
and to reflect your personal taste and style. I've been to dinner
parties where a host put three simple Granny Smith apples on
a wooden tray in the middle of the table with lots of little votive
candles around them. This was the centrepiece, and it looked
as beautiful as any gala floral arrangement at a fine hotel.

Sadly, the days of owning many different sets of china
are gone, mostly because our homes are smaller and few of
us have a household staff who can polish silver and tend to
the different sets of plates. Consequently, it's best to keep

your flatware and china simple. This will allow you to mix and match it with different centrepieces, flowers, tablecloths and napkins. I love white dishes for this very reason. As a butler and as a host, with these I can make a table look unique and appropriate no matter what the event.

Before you begin, think carefully and make decisions first, before actually doing anything. Often we will do things without thinking ahead and the end result will be less than perfect. Consider the following details:

- What is the purpose of the meal? Is it formal or informal; a meal for family or for business associates?
- How many guests will attend?
- What is the size of your table?
- What menu would work best? How many courses?
- What type of table service will you use?
- What is the style of your home, and of your flatware and tableware?

Take a methodical approach towards setting the table, beginning with an individual place setting and making sure every detail is in place. Once satisfied, set the rest of the table. In the end, your guests will notice and appreciate the overall effect.

TYPES OF TABLEWARE

When furnishing your table, go for simplicity. If you choose classic, elegant designs, your tableware will last you a lifetime, whereas if you choose complicated patterns or the trendy "colour of the season," your choices may go out of style quickly. Match styles so that your cutlery complements your dishes and your glassware. If you choose classic pieces, your table will always look good, no matter what price point you're buying at.

A note on crystal: it is expensive. And because glasses get broken over time, rarely do full sets get passed down from one generation to another. But drinking out of a crystal glass is so much nicer than drinking out of plain glass. And don't think that all your crystal glass sets have to match. You can have one set for cocktails and a different set (or two) at the table. My only word of caution is to keep all glasses within a set the same—for example, all your red wine glasses should be the same, and all the white wine glasses should be the same. You can mix and match, but still retain continuity. This makes collecting crystal glassware on sites like eBay or at yard sales easier. And when choosing between a purchase of large or small glasses, remember this: the larger the glass, the more people drink. So if you are budget-conscious, pick smaller glasses.

Here's where I have to confess that I have a china fetish. I love good china and think you can never have too much of it! But let's be reasonable: if it were not for my butler school, where I have the space to store different sets of china, I probably wouldn't have so much of it. My china collection at home is white so that I can mix and match based on textures— again, if you choose classic, it's hard to go wrong. This simplicity allows me to play with napkins and other table accessories.

Today, many people eschew silver because it's a lot of work to polish. When they think of silver, they remember that special occasion when they went into a cupboard, pulled out a silver tray or serving dish and realized to their horror that it was tarnished and couldn't be used. Cleaning a silver dish once it is fully tarnished is hard work—and I mean *really* hard work. And who wants to scrub silver on Christmas Eve or before a special celebration? But did you know that silver can be washed with hot water and a pH-neutral dish soap on a regular basis so that it doesn't tarnish and actually begins to build up a beautiful patina? (Yes, you will need to do one yearly polish, but that's it.)

Sadly, fewer sets are being manufactured today. But maybe this is the time to buy a vintage set, as they are reasonably priced, and when maintained properly they're beautiful and elegant.

SILVER PIECES

Below are some classic pieces that you would find in a traditional manor house or at a fine dinner. If you happen to discover any of these at a garage sale, my advice is to snap them up! Not only are they stunning on the table, they are lovely on display in your home.

SILVER TEA URN

This example is from the Victorian era. It does not have an independent heating source so water must be heated before it is poured in. Water must be replenished often so that it is always hot for service.

SILVER COFFEE POT

This beautiful coffee pot can be used anywhere coffee is being served, such as at the dining room table or in the living room.

SILVER HOT CHOCOLATE POT

Often mistaken for a coffee pot, this is in fact a hot chocolate pot/server. The hot chocolate should be made in a different vessel and then poured into this pre-heated serving pot before service.

CLARET JUG

Just like any other red wine, good claret should be decanted and any sediment left behind in the bottle. This is a typical claret jug made of glass or crystal.

CHAFING DISH

The silver chafing dish is often used today in the catering world; however, the British household used it for breakfast service. It works well for larger groups and for buffet-style service.

Often, chafing dishes have a heat source at the bottom and a reservoir for water. Fill the reservoir with hot water and light the heat source beneath to ensure that the chafing dish is good and hot before putting food into it for service.

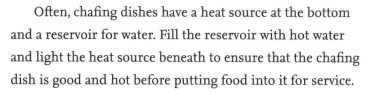

SAUCEBOAT

The sauceboat, or gravy boat, is passed around by guests at a table or presented by the butler. Traditionally, the sauceboat comes with a small oval saucer to catch any drips. Once the ladle has been put into the sauceboat, that is where it should remain during use, not on the saucer.

SERVING DISH AND COVER

Used for formal entertaining, this serving dish is for presenting venison, turkey, roast or other meats. The lid helps keep the food warm.

BASE OF A SERVING DISH

The base of the covered serving dish will have grooves to collect the juices from the meat.

FOLDING BISCUIT BOX

The Victorians loved biscuits, especially when they were served hot at the table. These are collectibles, but I do not see them in use often today. During the Victorian era, the butler would open the box so that each guest could pick a hot biscuit to eat with his or her meal.

CRUET

The cruet is a vessel used to hold condiments, such as mustard, oil and vinegar. Not often seen in use today, formal silver sets were made for the family table only, not for formal dinners.

THREE-TIER STAND

This stand is most commonly associated with afternoon tea. It can be used during afternoon tea or at a buffet. Most stands have dinner-sized plates that can go on each tier. This allows for easy replenishment.

MIRROR PLATEAU

Used to decorate the Georgian dining room table, these held everything from fresh fruit to flowers. They were mostly for decoration and display.

EPERGNE

This is a Victorian-style epergne. It is used for table decoration and for the display of flowers. Sometimes these are elaborate and placed on top of a mirrored plate. Combined with fresh-cut flowers from the garden, they made a great last-minute table centrepiece!

CANDLESTICK AND CANDELABRA

Candelabra are traditionally used either on the dining room table or on a serving side table. They look wonderful in pairs, depending on the length of the table.

CHINA

China manufacturers use no universal sizes or standards; however, here are some guidelines for purchasing china or planning which pieces to use for a reception.

BUTLER'S TIP

If you have spent a lot on your dishes, store them properly! Use felt liners between dishes to prevent scratches. If you don't have felt liners, a paper towel or a napkin will do the trick.

- Styles of china can be mixed as long as they are complementary and work well together.
- Plates of different shapes have different purposes and are suitable for different food items. When combining different plates and patterns, think about the effect for the person sitting at the table.
- Consider how plates will work for service. Plates with low rims are more difficult to clear, especially if set on chargers—a flat, decorative plate that sits under the dinner plate.

PLATES

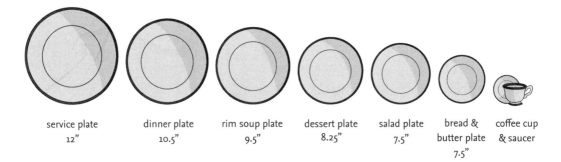

service plate 12"   dinner plate 10.5"   rim soup plate 9.5"   dessert plate 8.25"   salad plate 7.5"   bread & butter plate 7.5"   coffee cup & saucer

COFFEE AND TEA SERVICE

coffee pot   covered   milk or   teapot
sugar bowl   creamer

SERVING DISHES

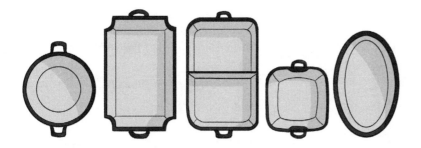

Left to right: chop plate (for pork, lamb or other chops), rectangular tray with handles, divided serving dish (usually for serving two kinds of vegetables), square cake plate, oval platter

---

THE BUTLER'S TOOLKIT: THE CHINA PANTRY

If, like me, you have a love of china that knows no bounds, consider making room in your house for a china pantry. In large estates, these are commonplace. Seeing all the china choices at once allows you to use different sets so you don't overuse just one.

SERVING BOWLS

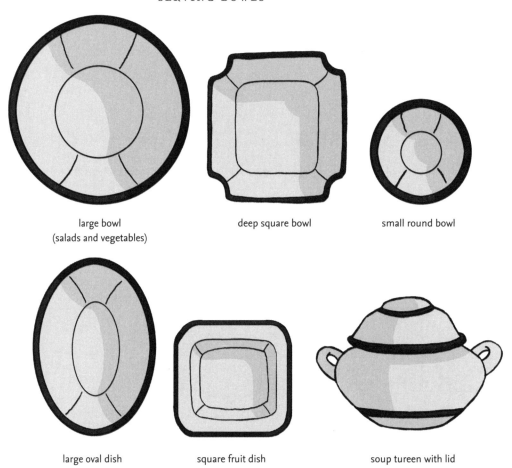

large bowl
(salads and vegetables)

deep square bowl

small round bowl

large oval dish

square fruit dish

soup tureen with lid

BUTLER'S TIP

Most serving dishes are multipurpose. Just because a divided serving
dish is usually used to serve two kinds of vegetables doesn't mean you
can't use it at breakfast to serve two kinds of fruit.

CUTLERY

From the days when everyone used to carry around a knife and spoon to parties to today, when the host or hostess has a full set of cutlery, here is a description of all the pieces you need to know.

FORKS

seafood · snail · oyster · pastry · salad · dessert · fish · luncheon · main course

KNIVES

butter · fruit · fish · luncheon / dessert · steak · dinner

SPOONS

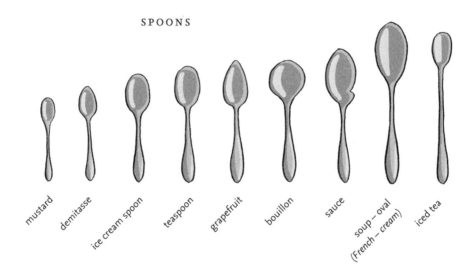

mustard

demitasse

ice cream spoon

teaspoon

grapefruit

bouillon

sauce

soup – oval
(French – cream)

iced tea

SERVING UTENSILS

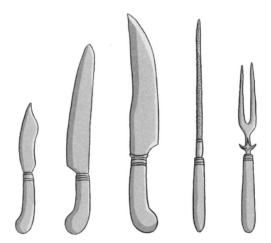

Left to right: butter knife, cake knife, knife and steel, carving fork

Left to right: cheese knife, planer, stilton spoon

Left to right: three sizes of soup ladles, punch ladle

Left to right: meat fork, fish fork, fish knife, pasta server, pasta fork, pastry skewer, cake server

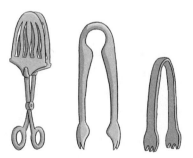

Left to right: pastry tongs, ice cube tongs, sugar tongs

GLASSWARE

The bigger the glass, the more people drink. If you want to be economical, use small wineglasses.

red wine 16 oz white wine 12.5 oz champagne flute 8 oz water goblet 14.5 oz ice wine or sherry 4 oz

Collins glass: This is traditionally used for a Tom Collins or iced tea. This glass is very tall and narrow.

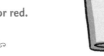

Highball glass: This is the most commonly used glass for large mixed drinks.

Double Old-Fashioned: This is the most commonly used glass for smaller mixed drinks or for liquor served either on the rocks or straight up.

TABLE-SETTING PROCESS

While fashion in table settings has changed over the centuries, affecting the flatware, glassware and china we use, the method of setting a table remains exactly the same.

This is the basic method I recommend:

1. Set just one place setting first. Don't try to set the entire table at once as there will just be more to undo if you don't like how it looks. Make sure the placement is correct and that you are happy with it.

2. Next, take the rest of the chargers or main course plates and place them around the table where you want to set all the other place settings. Keep the spacing between settings equidistant. Once they are properly positioned, organize utensils and glassware around them.

3. Check for symmetry. Why do we care so much about this? Because the human eye loves symmetry. When things are not symmetrical our eye sees imperfection. Use the butler stick for this! (See p. 106)

Below, I include four different styles of place setting. Each is subtly different from the next. Interestingly, most cultures eat using utensils, and most also begin with utensils on the outside of a place setting, working inward towards the plate.

THE AMERICAN PLACE SETTING

In this setting, the glasses form a diamond shape above the cutlery, with the first glass placed directly above the main course knife (inside, right). The dessert spoon and the fork are at the top of the plate, and above them is the place card. Guests use the cutlery from the outside moving in. This place setting starts with a soup course (spoon, outside right), moves on to a salad (fork, outside left), a fish course (middle fork and knife) and a meat course (inside fork and knife).

THE EUROPEAN PLACE SETTING

In this setting, the glasses are placed on a diagonal on the right of the plate. Individual salt and pepper shakers are placed above the plate. The spoon (outside, right) is for the first course, soup. The next fork and knife are for the second course (fish), and the final inside set is for the main meat course. The fork closest to the plate is for salad, which in this meal will be served last. Cutlery for dessert will be offered later. Sometimes it is placed closest to the plate, though not in this drawing.

THE CHINESE PLACE SETTING

In China, there is no standard for formal place settings at tables as is common practice in the Western world. In fact, the focus is on the food rather than the place setting. The diagram shows a typical place setting, but it can easily be changed to suit your needs without making any errors of etiquette.

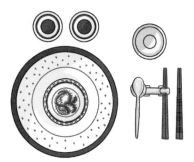

THE FRENCH PLACE SETTING

Traditionally, the French place setting in a residence does not include a bread and butter plate, or a knife for the salad course. And although the cutlery is laid out the same way as in American and British settings, the forks and spoons are turned over. The reason? French family monograms are engraved on the back of the cutlery, so it's placed face down to show that it's real silver.

BUTLER'S TIP

A trend in Chinese table settings is to provide two sets of chopsticks: the set that rests beside the soup spoon is for personal use, and the outer set is used by guests when helping themselves to communal food.

USING A BUTLER STICK TO PREPARE
A PLACE SETTING

One of the first rules of formal table setting is the 24-inch rule. This refers to the ideal amount of space from the centre of one plate to the centre of the next plate, allowing the guest plenty of elbow room. The two pictures that follow illustrate this. You may need to decrease the distance if your table is not large enough to allow 24 inches between.

The ideal distance from the back of a chair to the edge of the table is also 24 inches. This allows guests to sit comfortably. A good butler will use his or her butler stick to take these two measurements.

Today, few people use butler sticks to set their daily dinner tables, and to be truthful, even the contemporary butler doesn't necessarily use the tool every day. But when there is a special occasion—such as an important family birthday or anniversary—the butler stick could be of use.

This is how a professional butler would set the dining table with a butler stick.

Step 1:
Align the bottom of the butler stick with the edge of the table. The baseline for a place setting should be about one inch from the edge of the table—the width of the butler stick.

Step 2:

Align all the cutlery, the plate and the napkin to touch the top of the butler stick. This will create the perfect straight edge for your place setting. The plate should be centred at the 0, the centre of the butler stick.

Step 3:

Ideally, place the first knife 1 to 1.5 inches away from the plate. Continue using this same metric for the rest of the cutlery so that it is all equidistant. Note: you may choose to reduce the amount of space between items of cutlery if your table space is limited. What's important is to keep everything consistent.

Step 4:

As you move around the table creating each place setting, use the same measurements.

Step 5:

To help achieve a beautiful place setting, strive for accuracy, and horizontal and vertical symmetry.

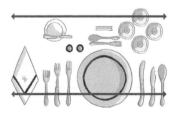

NAPKIN FOLDING

In Victorian and Edwardian times, fancier napkin folds were the mark of well-trained and sophisticated household staff. As the hotel industry flourished in the 20th century, fancy napkin folds remained important and continued to suggest refinement. This was one of the ways hotels mimicked the sophistication of aristocratic estates.

As beautiful as these napkin folds are, the modern trend is towards a simpler style. In fact, overly intricate folds may be seen as a sign of a lack of sophistication, and even as unhygienic: a professional butler will do everything in his power to avoid touching your napkin, and that includes keeping the fold as simple as possible. Wait staff in modern restaurants, however, sometimes place napkins on the laps of their patrons. This difference in etiquette is one that tells me whether someone has been trained by a hotel or in butler school.

Having said this, there are some beautiful napkin folds that are appropriate for special occasions. Below are eight folds that I use regularly. My all-time favourite, a fold I use over and over both for its simplicity and elegance, is the monogram napkin fold.

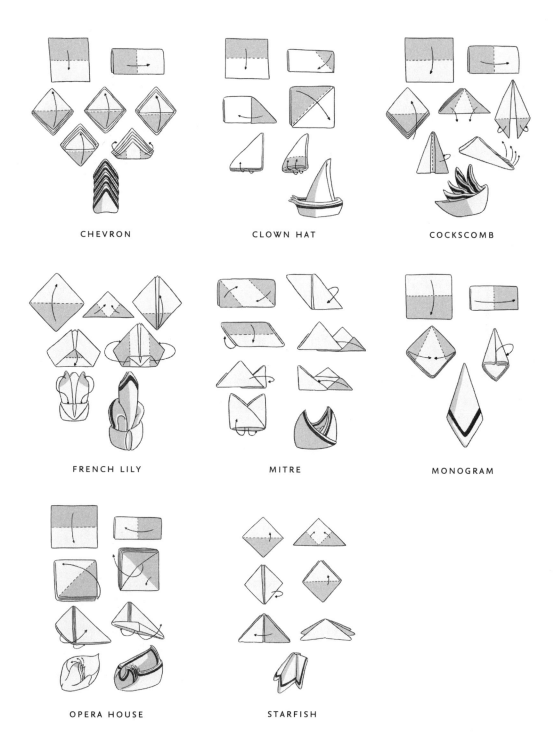

CHEVRON

CLOWN HAT

COCKSCOMB

FRENCH LILY

MITRE

MONOGRAM

OPERA HOUSE

STARFISH

MENU CARDS

Not all events require a menu card, and the more casual ones certainly do not. It would seem a tad pretentious to prepare a menu card for a family dinner by the pool with your neighbours. So when are they appropriate? If many courses are being served, the card allows guests to pace themselves. Also, a guest may be allergic to or simply dislike a certain dish, and a menu card will allow them to avoid it without awkwardness. Menu cards remove the element of surprise, and are a courtesy for your guests.

Folded Menu Card

MENU CARD STYLES

There are two basic types of menu card styles. The folded card is the more formal of the two. A single flat card may also be used for formal occasions, or for casual occasions if written in an informal manner.

Flat Menu Card

HOW TO CORRECTLY WRITE A MENU CARD

The simple format of a menu card has not changed over time. (See the illustration on the next page for the most common format.) When writing a menu card, keep your language clear. It is pretentious to use foreign-language descriptions on an English menu card unless citing the proper name of a dish—for example, *coq au vin*.

Generally, place the menu on the right side of a folded menu card; however, if the folded card also includes the evening's program, then place the menu on the left side with the program on the right side. Menu cards may be printed or typed. For personal events, they may even be handwritten.

Include the following information:

- name of the host
- household name and/or date
- the title "Menu"
- course listings in the order they will be served, with matching beverages
- post-dinner menu (e.g., in the sample shown, *Coffee, served in the library*)

Mr. and Mrs. Jones

RIDEAU HOUSE
Menu

Cream Soup of Wild Turkey
Veuve Clicquot Ponsardin 1999

~

Salad of Seasonal Greens

~

Steamed Whole Trout
Gewürztraminer, Hugel et Fils 2003

~

Beef Wellington
Glazed Miniature Carrots
Dauphine Potatoes
Green Beans Amandine
Château Leoville 1996

~

Bananas Foster

~

Coffee
Served in the library

Traditionally, a menu card is positioned on the guest's napkin or in an individual menu-card holder above the place setting. Menu cards should never lean against any of the glasses in a place setting.

If you are providing a few handwritten menu cards for people to share, these can be arranged in a menu-card holder in the centre of the table. If you have only one menu card, it should be placed in front of the host or hostess, allowing him or her to discuss the menu with guests.

THE BUTLER'S TOOLKIT: SEATING BOARD

The seating board is traditionally used for formal dinner receptions and is either held by the butler at the entrance of the dining room or placed on the side table. This allows guests to see where they are to be seated and the butler to direct them efficiently. In my experience, this puts the guests at ease. Even when using a seating board, provide place cards on the table at each individual place setting.

TYPES OF TABLE SERVICE

With so many different cultures around the world, many different forms of table service have been used, modified and, alas, performed incorrectly. Below, I have listed the seven types of table service and given parameters for when to employ each.

- Host/hostess
- Plate
- Family Style
- Buffet
- Butler or French Service
- Service au Gueridon
- Russian or Silver Service

HOST/HOSTESS

Originating in Britain, this type of service requires the host or hostess to serve the meal. The plates and food are placed in front of one or the other, and he or she serves the food onto guests' plates. Once the individual plate has been prepared, it is then passed around the table from guest to guest until it reaches its recipient. Or the butler takes each plate from the host and brings it to the intended guest. This style is slow but highly personal and ideal for an intimate meal with close family and friends. If the table seats more than six, however, it's not the best service to choose because the food will get cold while guests wait to be served.

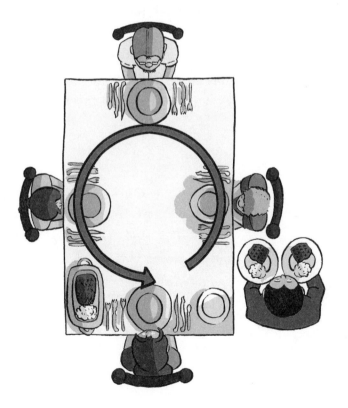

BUTLER'S TIP

In North America, when a served plate is passed around the table, it always goes in a counter-clockwise direction.

PLATE

Plate service is simple and the most commonly used method. Warm dinner plates are fully dressed and garnished in the kitchen. Once the chef says the plates are ready, they are brought to the table. A proper butler will carry a maximum of two plates at a time, one in each hand. He or she will serve the full plate with the left hand and remove dishes with the right. When clearing dishes, again a butler should never hold more than two plates.

FAMILY STYLE

This is a typical method for meals with your family or friends. The butler places warm empty plates in front of each guest. The butler or host/hostess then places platters of food in the centre of the table with the service utensils beside or on each platter. Guests then help themselves.

BUFFET

Buffet service is considered by many to be a cheap form of entertaining lavishly, but I have never understood this. In fact it requires a good quantity of food to make the buffet appear full. For a buffet to succeed, the food should be

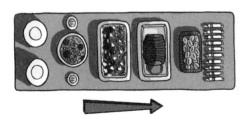

replenished regularly. You don't want your last guests serving themselves to be left standing there and looking at picked-over platters. Note that to work efficiently, a buffet line should always move in one direction.

BUTLER SERVICE OR FRENCH SERVICE

This method of service is not common, but it is traditional and it's one I like. The butler places warm dinner plates in front of each guest. The butler then moves around the table with a platter of food. The serving utensils are positioned on the platter facing the guest. The butler carefully approaches each guest from the left and offers the platter, and the guest helps him or herself to the food.

This service is appealing because guests can take as much or as little as they want. It is slower, however, than some other service methods. Remember that food should be cut into pieces that are easy for guests to serve onto their plates.

SERVICE AU GUERIDON

Most commonly used in high-end restaurants, this method of service is a dying art. It is, however, beautiful and entertaining for guests. The chef or an experienced butler prepares a dish in front of guests on a trolley beside the table. Examples of foods served this way include salads and dessert crepes.

My most memorable experience of French service was in a restaurant where the chef made a sauce from scratch for the main course of beef tournedos. What made this so special was that the chef actually let the guests taste the sauce to make sure it was to our liking before drizzling it on the beef. Now that's service!

RUSSIAN SERVICE OR SILVER SERVICE

Used often at formal dinner parties, this method is similar to butler service with one slight difference. The butler first places warm dinner plates in front of guests, then brings a platter of food to the table and serves each guest. It is most polite if the butler asks the guest what he or she would like from the platter.

FOUR STYLES OF SERVING AT TABLE

AMERICAN STYLE

The waiter should approach the guest from behind, and serve the food to guests from the left. Empty or dirty plates are always removed from the guest's right, and beverages are served from the right side as well.

DINER STYLE

Rather informal, this style makes for a warm, homey dining experience, similar to the service at an all-American diner. For this type of service, the butler stands at the edge of the table and will either pass the full plates to individual guests or, in situations where the butler cannot physically reach the guest, he or she might pass the plate to the nearest guest, who then passes it on to the next. This style works best for small dinner parties.

EUROPEAN STYLE OR ENGLISH STYLE

The waiter approaches the guest from behind, and all service takes place from the right-hand side. This differs from American Style in that the empty dishes are removed from the right as well.

MILITARY STYLE

This very formal style of service is beautiful to watch when done correctly. A waiter carries no more than two plates, and all waiters enter the dining room in single file. The waiters circle the table, and each waiter stands behind one female guest. At the head waiter's signal, each woman around the table is served at the same time. The process is repeated for the gentlemen guests as well. All the waiters leave the room together, in the same order as they entered. Military Style is costly because it requires a large number of staff members, and it also takes time, but it is by far the most striking way to serve your guests.

FROM THE DAYS OF KING ARTHUR at the beginning of the medieval era, the round table was well established as a symbol of community. The most important item on it was the salt, and it was placed in front of the highest-ranking person.

At that time, when the only utensils used at the table were spoons and knives, hosts did not provide the place settings. Instead, those attending a meal were expected to bring their own utensils. The tradition of the silver spoon dates back to this epoch. If you were from a wealthy family, when you were baptized by your godparents you were given a silver spoon—hence the expression "born with a silver spoon in one's mouth." Those not born into wealth could not afford the luxury of silver and instead used spoons made of tinned iron. Food was prepared and placed in the centre of the table and guests would help themselves. Whatever scraps they didn't want were thrown to the ground, where dogs and cats would eat them. Napkins had not been invented, so guests simply wiped their hands on the hem of the tablecloth.

Table manners evolved during the Renaissance. Napkins and music at the table became all the rage in high society. The fork first appeared in Italy, but amidst much tumult. The Church and the public initially protested this utensil because it was perceived as somewhat vulgar and rude. But, by the time Charles II was restored to the throne in 1660, forks were here to stay. Forks were an important invention, not just because they were practical, but because using them was more hygienic than eating with one's hands. Later, this movement towards improved hygiene led to better table linens, finer cloth and the birth of the napkin.

Queen Anne of England ascended the throne on May 1, 1707. She loved anything to do with the dining table and gastronomy. The "Queen Anne Period" was particularly prosperous and the queen, along with her friend Sarah Jennings, the first Duchess of Marlborough, hired silversmiths all over the United Kingdom who crafted items and developed amenities specifically for the table.

The setting of tables has progressed over time, and while fashions come and go, the importance of people gathering to eat together remains the same. Manners will continue to evolve, but we will always have a special reverence for the communal breaking of bread.

CARVING

Carving in the privacy of the kitchen, in the dining room or on view in front of your employers and their guests can be stressful, particularly if you are not confident in your carving ability. The following sections will demystify the process and help you understand the anatomy of meat, bones and joints so that you can become a master of the art of carving—no matter where you choose to do it.

Here are a few pointers:

• Keep a sharp knife in hand and stay focused on the task.
• When in doubt, cut against the grain of the meat.
• Let the meat rest at least 20 minutes before carving.
• Practise, practise, practise!

CARVING EQUIPMENT

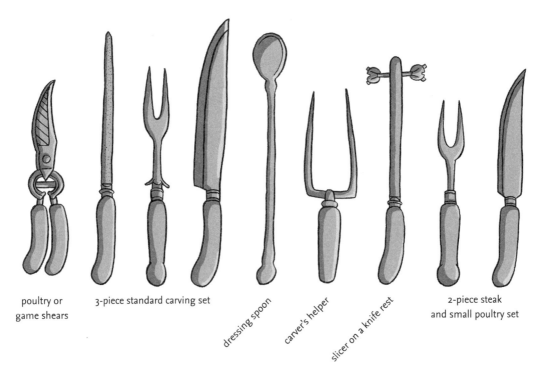

poultry or
game shears

3-piece standard carving set

dressing spoon

carver's helper

slicer on a knife rest

2-piece steak
and small poultry set

ROLLED ROAST

Step 1: Lay the rolled roast on its end.

Step 2: Carve across the grain horizontally in thin, even slices. Remove each slice and place on either a heated serving platter or a dinner plate. Note: the first slice should be served only to someone who prefers meat well cooked. Any strings should be removed as you carve.

CROWN ROAST

Step 1: Remove the strings from the roast. Insert the carving fork into the side of the roast to steady it and begin cutting in a downward motion between ribs to slice into chops.

Step 2: Remove the chops and place on either a heated serving platter or a dinner plate.

STANDING RIB ROAST

Step 1: Lay the rib roast with the largest end down. Insert the carving fork below the first rib to hold the roast steady. Carve across the grain horizontally, starting from the outside edge and slicing towards the bones.

Step 2: To release the top slice from the bone, use the tip of the knife to slice down, cutting close to the bone.

Step 3: Remove the top slice and place on either a heated serving platter or a dinner plate. Continue to slice horizontally and downward.

HAM, BONE-IN

Step 1: Cut a piece off the ham leaving a solid flat base.

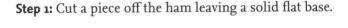

Step 2: Turn the ham onto the flat base and begin carving even slices in a downward motion to the bone.

Step 3: Once you have cut as many slices as you need, cut at the base of the slices horizontally along the bone to remove the slices. Place slices on either a heated serving platter or a dinner plate.

PORTERHOUSE STEAK

Step 1: Separate the meat from the bone. To do this, hold the meat steady with the carving fork and cut closely around the bone with the tip of the knife.

Step 2: Continue cutting all around the centre bone on all sides.

Step 3: Remove the bone from the meat. The porterhouse steak consists of two cuts of meat. The larger side is the striploin and the smaller side is the tenderloin.

Step 4: Begin slicing at the bone end of the steak and cut the porterhouse steak straight down into even 1-inch slices or cut on a slight angle into ½-inch slices. Serve a slice of each cut to every guest.

RACK ROAST

Step 1: Place the rack meat side down.

Step 2: If the rack has not been trimmed of the chine bone (backbone), use the carving fork to hold it steady so you can cut it off. Removing the chine bone will make carving easier.

Step 3: Begin cutting in a downward motion between ribs to slice into chops. Remove the chops and place on either a heated serving platter or a dinner plate.

ROAST LEG OF LAMB, BONE-IN

Step 1: Cut a piece off the roast leaving a solid flat base.

Step 2: Turn the roast onto the flat base and begin carving even slices (1/4-inch to 1/2-inch thick) in a downward motion to the bone.

Step 3: Once you have cut as many slices as you need, cut at the base of the slices horizontally along the bone to remove the slices. Place slices on either a heated serving platter or a dinner plate.

TURKEY

Step 1: Start by removing the legs one at a time using the two-prong carving fork to hold the leg in place. As you cut the skin around the leg, use the fork to pull the leg away from the breast to expose the hip joint. Cut through this joint to remove the leg.

Step 2: Place the leg on a plate. Cut through the joint to separate the thigh from the drumstick. Slice the meat off the bone. Place on either a heated serving platter or a dinner plate.

Step 3: Remove the wings one at a time using the two-pronged carving fork to hold each wing. With the fork, pull the wing slightly away from the breast to expose the shoulder joint. Cut through this joint to remove the wing.

Step 4: Hold the turkey steady with the carving fork as you cut the breast meat parallel to the breastbone in long, even, thin slices. Place slices on a heated serving platter or dinner plate.

Step 5: Remove stuffing from the cavity of the bird and place in a heated serving bowl.

HOW TO PREPARE A CHEESE PLATE

Cheese is more popular today than ever. Although cheese was commonly served at the dining table as its own course, the relaxed formalities of today mean the cheese course at the dinner table is rather rare. It has now become popular during the cocktail hour at parties.

Cheese as part of the hors d'oeuvres course is wonderful. Once served, it does not require any further effort from the host or hostess, and guests can help themselves. The most important detail when serving cheese is to serve it at room temperature! Most cheese plates have just come out of the refrigerator and are too cold. A cold brie has no flavour, but a

The blade of a cheese knife is narrow at the handle and widens towards the tip. Use the forked end to pick up the sliced cheese.

room-temperature brie that has been out of the refrigerator for a few hours comes alive and is a delicacy. Cheese will not go bad quickly, so don't worry about that. When slicing cheese for yourself, include both the heart and the rind so that everyone gets an equal share of the various flavours.

The way cheese is served largely depends on its shape. Here are some sample cheeses and recommended methods for cutting.

Pont-l'Évêque

A square cheese, this has a white-orange rind and is rich and soft, with a creamy, full-bodied flavour.

Tomme

Tomme can be made from cow's milk or goat's milk. The taste varies from nutty to citrusy depending on the type of milk used. The texture ranges from semi-soft to crumbly.

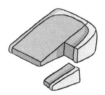

Brie

This cow's milk cheese has an edible, soft white rind. The taste ranges from light and delicate to rich and buttery.

Camembert

This traditional French cheese from the Normandy region has a soft edible rind with a delicate nutty and mild salty taste.

Charolles

Also called Charolais, this barrel-shaped, semi-soft cheese from the Burgundy region can be made from goat's milk, cow's milk or a blend of both. It has a salty-sweet taste.

Picodon

This soft goat's milk cheese from the Rhône-Alpes region has a mild flavour. With age, the texture becomes crumbly and the flavour more pronounced.

Valençay

A pyramid-shaped goat's milk cheese, Valençay has a smooth and dense texture, with a mild lemony taste.

Epoisses

Made in the Burgundy region of France, this pungent, creamy-textured cow's milk cheese is rich and salty.

Emmental

This traditional Swiss cheese has a firm, smooth texture with a mild to nutty flavour.

CHEESE PLATE PRESENTATION

When you make a cheese platter, you should present a variety of soft cheese (such as brie) and hard cheese (such as an aged cheddar). Include a mild cheese as well (such as Valençay), and a strong or sharp cheese (such as blue cheese). You won't be able to dictate how your guests sample your cheeses, but when eating cheese yourself, always start with the mildest variety and work your way towards the strongest. Going the opposite way may overwhelm your palate and you won't be able to enjoy the milder flavours.

A beautiful cheese plate presentation says everything about you as a host. Small plates and cocktail napkins are always appealing. When preparing a cheese service, set out one knife per cheese, fresh fruit (grapes, for instance) and plenty of complementary crackers or breads. Whatever breads or crackers you provide, they should be fresh. If you're serving soft cheeses, a nice white French baguette is perfect. A stronger cheese calls for a heartier bread, like a rustic farmer's loaf. Include one type of whole-grain bread and one white bread option as well. And offer a variety of crackers. If possible, identify the different cheeses.

BUTLER'S TIP

When arranging a cheese plate, cut just a few slices of bread at a time. Bread can go stale quickly, so leave out the loaf and a cutting board for guests to help themselves.

HOW TO SET UP THE PERFECT BAR

These are the two worst things that can happen when you've set up a bar at a function: a) you run out of alcohol or mix, and b) you run out of ice. Make sure you have enough of each for the size of your party.

Here is a good basic checklist to help you put together your perfect bar, for any occasion. Feel free to make changes based on your crowd. You know their drinking habits better than I do! I leave the brands to your discretion.

❏ Rye

❏ Scotch

❏ Rum

❏ Vodka

❏ Gin

❏ Whisky

❏ Vermouth – dry

❏ Vermouth – sweet

❏ Wine – white

❏ Wine – red

❏ Champagne/Sparkling Wine

❏ Orange juice

❏ Tomato juice

❏ Cranberry juice

❏ Pink Grapefruit juice

❏ Cognac

❏ Baileys

❏ Grand Marnier liqueur

❏ Cointreau

❏ Coffee liqueur

❏ Water – sparkling

❏ Water – flat

❏ Cola

❏ Ginger Ale

❏ Soda water

❏ Tonic water

❏ Ice

❏ Olives

❏ Lemons & limes

BAR ACCESSORIES

These are the must-haves for your bar. You can add other items depending on the preferences of your guests.

Champagne stopper

Perfect for keeping the leftover champagne bubbly! Some stoppers can also be used for wine bottles.

Standard cocktail shaker

Invented by an innkeeper in the 1800s, this is used to mix ingredients for cocktails.

Measure

Also called a jigger or pony, it is used to measure cocktail ingredients—especially alcohol.

Bar spoon

The bar spoon is for reaching inside a standard shaker and stirring. Think of James Bond when a martini is being made, although, of course, he would not want it stirred with a bar spoon.

Mixing glass

Attach this glass to the top of a standard shaker when making fizzy cocktails.

Grater

Most often used for creating garnishes for cocktails, like a sliver of lemon rind or a shaving of chocolate.

Hawthorne strainer

Use this strainer to hold back the ice when pouring mixed cocktails into an appropriate glass.

Wine corkscrew

Also called a waiter's friend or sommelier knife, it is used for drawing the cork out of a wine bottle. The blade is used to cut the foil around the neck of some bottles.

Muddler

This is for mixing the ingredients and crushing them to release the flavours, for instance mint in a mojito.

BASIC MIXOLOGY TECHNIQUES

Chilling a Glass

Put the glass in the freezer for a few hours before use. If you are short of time, fill the glass with crushed ice and let the ice sit for a few minutes or swirl it around. Dump the ice when the drink is ready to be poured.

Fresh versus Canned Juice

Whenever possible, use freshly squeezed juice. This is simple with a good commercial juicer, and it will make a huge difference to the quality of your bar drinks. If you're preparing freshly squeezed juices ahead of time, however, be aware that after twenty-four hours the flavour starts to deteriorate. Three basic juices to have on hand are orange, grapefruit and tomato. If you do not have time to make fresh juice, purchase a good-quality juice at your local grocer.

Mixing Drinks Containing Fruit Juices
Pour the fruit juice before adding the liquor to ensure thorough mixing.

Adding a Twist of Lemon
Rub a narrow strip of peel around the rim of the glass to deposit the oil. Twist the peel so that the oil (usually one small drop) escapes into the drink and then drop the peel into the drink.

BUTLER'S TIP

Whenever I decant wine, I set a large outdoor flashlight on the counter aimed at the bottle's neck so that I can see the sediment. It might not be as romantic as using a candle, but it's more effective.

DECANTING A BOTTLE OF WINE

When you order a bottle of wine at a restaurant, a good server will have you taste it before he or she pours the glasses. A household butler, however, would never present wine to his employers and ask them to try it at the table. Tasting is the job of the butler and done before dinner is served.

When serving wine in your home, first uncork and taste it, preferably away from your guests. If the bottle passes muster, you can then decant it and prepare it for the table.

Step 1: Stand the bottle up for a few days before opening to let any sediment settle to the bottom.

Step 2: Holding the bottle gently, use the cutter on your corkscrew to remove the top of the foil.

Step 3: Insert the tip of the corkscrew into the middle of the cork and then turn the handle until the screw won't go any farther into the cork.

Step 4: Move the lever arm down, so that it is flush against the neck of the bottle.

Step 5: Pull up on the handle firmly to remove the cork.

Step 6: When decanting the wine, position a light source below the bottle—that way, you'll see when the sediment is about to reach the lip. That's when you stop pouring.

OPENING A BOTTLE OF CHAMPAGNE

Step 1: Remove all of the foil from a well-chilled bottle of champagne.

Step 2: With your thumb placed firmly on top of the cork, twist off the wire cage open.

Step 3: With your thumb still firmly on the cork and wire cage, slowly twist the bottle from the base with your other hand until you feel the cork release.

Step 4: Pour a little of the champagne into each flute. This is called "priming the glass."

Step 5: Let the bubbles subside before you fill the rest of each glass 3/4 full.

BUILDING A CHAMPAGNE TOWER

I know a champagne tower requires more work than most people want to put into a dinner party. But if you know how to make one, you can do it as a treat when you're hosting a party! It's beautiful to look at, and adds a festive touch to any gathering. Remember that the glasses are wet on the outside because of the champagne dripping down, so be careful when serving not to get champagne on anyone. And, as a side note, the champagne tower can only be done using champagne saucers, not flutes.

Step 1: Build the champagne tower on a sturdy table using champagne saucers.

Step 2: Determine the total number of glasses you need, and then calculate the number of glasses for the base.

Step 3: Align the glasses to form a square.

Step 4: Place the glasses so that the outer edges touch one another. If this is done correctly, you'll see a diamond-shaped space between each cluster of four glasses.

Step 5: Place the second row of glasses so that the stems are centred over the diamond-shaped spaces.

 **Step 6:** Repeat the process.

 **Step 7:** Carefully build the tower.

 **Step 8:** Ensure each glass is properly aligned.

 **Step 9:** A finished champagne tower should look like this.

 **Step 10:** Pour champagne in the top glass so that it trickles down into glasses on lower tiers. Continue to pour until the bottom tier of glasses is filled.

CLEANING CRYSTAL

Few things sparkle as brightly as a perfectly clean crystal goblet. Think of the feeling you get when you walk into a restaurant and see all the crystal glasses catching the light. Now think of how horrible it would be for one of your guests to look more closely at one of your glasses and see a lipstick smudge! Never fear, dear reader. This can easily be avoided if you use the proper technique to clean your crystal.

Step 1: Wash glass by hand in moderately hot water with a small amount of pH-neutral dish soap.

Step 2: Rinse well in clean moderately hot water. Place upside down on linen to dry.

Step 3: For extra shine, steam over boiling water, then place upside down on linen to dry.

Step 4: Have at the ready two clean, dry linen tea towels.

Step 5: First, hold glass by base and polish.

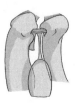

DON'T

Step 6: Use left hand to cradle the bowl and polish with your right hand. Never twist the base and bowl when washing or drying the inside of the glass.

Step 7: The perfect result.

BUTLER'S TIP

Always use a 100 percent cotton dishcloth to dry your dishes, as it will absorb moisture much better than a blended fabric cloth.

WASHING DISHES

In the homes of the Victorians and Edwardians, scullery maids had the hard task of washing the dishes after every meal. Today, many homes have the luxury of a dishwasher— and what a pleasure that is! If you don't have a dishwasher, though, I'll let you in on a little secret: washing dishes by hand is easy. And, as any good butler knows, even if you use a dishwasher, it's best to rinse your dishes with a pH-neutral soap and hot water before putting them in the machine because they will come out cleaner this way.

Step 1: Dishes can be washed directly in the sink or in a separate washtub. If you're washing dishes in the sink, place a rubber mat on the bottom. This avoids chipping or breaking dishes while washing them.

Step 2: Scrape off any food left on the dishes and lightly rinse. Place the dishes in the sink or a washtub filled with hot soapy water. Dip a sponge in the soapy water and gently scrub away food and residue.

Step 3: Rinse the dishes thoroughly in clean, hot water to remove the soap.

Step 4: Place the washed items on the dish rack to drain off excess water. Don't overcrowd the dish rack.

Step 5: Dry thoroughly with a clean cotton towel.

BUTLER'S TIP

When putting away clean dishes, place them at the bottom or back of the cupboard.
This ensures that the same dishes are not being used over and over again.

HOW TO LOAD A DISHWASHER

A dishwasher used effectively works wonders, but as soon as something blocks the flow of water around and between dishes, efficiency is compromised. Remember that for the cleaning cycle to work effectively, the dish water must circulate around each item. Overcrowding leads to less-than-spotless dishes and unsatisfying results.

Some people try to save money on soap, but this is not something on which you should cut back. Use the manufacturer's recommended amount. Also spend time, if necessary, figuring out the best soap for your dishwasher, and for the type of water provided in your area. Liquid and powder dish soaps react differently based on the type of water.

This illustration shows the best placement of dishes in a dishwasher. Note the amount of space around the dishes, which allows for good water flow.

THE CUTLERY TRAY

The cutlery in the tray should point upward. This allows for maximum water circulation. Don't put all the knives in one compartment and forks in another. It's better to mix it up.

HOW TO CLEAN STAINLESS STEEL CUTLERY

Few homeowners today use silver cutlery on a daily basis. Stainless steel flatware comes in so many styles that there's something for every decor, and it's dishwasher safe. But here are some tips for cleaning your stainless steel flatware properly.

- Place flatware in the cutlery basket of the dishwasher with handles pointing down and knife and fork tips pointing up.
- To remove water spots on the flatware after dishwashing, use a soft, lint-free cloth dampened with vinegar.
- As with china and glassware, rotate flatware so that the same pieces are not being used repeatedly. Place the cleanest flatware at the bottom of the storage tray.
- Never put stainless steel and silver into a dishwasher together, as the metals can react negatively to each other. And, be careful of the handles—if there is bone or another delicate material on the handle, be sure to hand wash it.
- Never place carving knives in the dishwasher. To ensure that the blades stay as sharp as possible, they should always be hand washed.

POLISHING SILVER

There are few dining items that look as marvellous as polished, gleaming silver. And cleaning it properly is easier than most people believe, provided you do it often. When silver isn't cleaned regularly, tarnish builds up, making cleaning more labour-intensive than it needs to be.

The following steps, and a little elbow grease, will have your silver pieces looking beautiful again.

Step 1: While wearing clean dish gloves, rinse the silverware with fresh warm water.

Step 2: Wet a clean sponge, and pour a good amount of silver polish onto it.

Step 3: Rub the entire surface of the item with the sponge and silver cleaner. Add more cleaner to your sponge if necessary.

Step 4: If possible, use only the sponge to clean the silver, as it's gentle and won't damage the surface. But for difficult areas, you can use a soft, clean toothbrush with a little silver cleaner on the bristles—but only to get into those nooks and crannies.

Step 5: Thoroughly rinse the silver item so no polish remains.

Step 6: Dry immediately with a cotton towel, and then rub with a buffing cloth until you see a beautiful shine.

BUTLER'S TIP

The more you use your silver, the less it will need to be polished!
Also, a pH-neutral soap will help preserve its lustre.

Part Four

Table Manners
for the 21ST Century

MY PARENTS ARE VIGILANT of my table manners. Every time they watch me eat chicken with a knife and fork (the only method allowed in our house), they instruct me as if I were still eight years old. I sometimes tease my mother and say, "Mom, it's really hard being your best child and having to do everything properly!" And my mother always responds, "Charles, you are my *only* child, so this gives you the privilege of also being my *best* and my *worst* child."

Despite our table banter, I am grateful to both of my parents for teaching me etiquette as a child (and even today!). Table manners are as important now as they ever were. For starters, people judge us based on our table manners. When we eat in an unmannerly way, others are taken aback—and sometimes even disgusted. The opposite is true when we exhibit good manners. It's a way to socialize with others. Despite my parents' opinions, people often compliment me on how I am able to eat chicken wings with a knife and fork and remove all the meat.

In a business setting, if you take clients to lunch, think about how important your table manners are. You represent your company, so your social skills should be top-notch. Table manners are so important that some universities, such as MIT, offer short etiquette classes to prepare students for the job market. And some law firms take prospective candidates out for lunch as part of the final interview process and judge them in part on how they eat, drink and speak at the table. As potential employers, they want to know if a candidate will be able to entertain important clients without embarrassing themselves or the firm.

Throughout history, food has often been scarce. Sharing food with guests was a big deal and one's wealth was defined by how much food one had on the table. Today, food may be more plentiful for most of us living in developed countries, but good-quality food is still hard to get and tends to be expensive. There is still significance in preparing and serving a meal, and for those invited to a table—to *any* table, grand or not—and table manners are a way of showing respect and gratitude, not to mention grace.

Of course, table manners vary based on culture and country. What is acceptable in one culture may not be so in another. A perfect example of this is the difference between the French and British way of eating soup. The British tip their soup plates away from themselves, whereas the French tip their dishes towards themselves. Does this mean that one method is right and one wrong? Of course not. But when travelling, one should be aware and respectful of cultural differences.

Do not feel obligated to conform to foreign table manners, however, unless you are comfortable with the practice. If you have never used chopsticks in your life and find yourself at dinner with friends or clients at a Japanese restaurant, using chopsticks incorrectly could cause you and your meal partners embarrassment. Instead, ask discreetly for a knife and fork. When you host an event or dinner, it's very important to never assume. Just because you are entertaining someone who isn't Japanese doesn't mean they don't know how to use chopsticks. Consequently, having only a fork and knife at their place setting might be insulting. To err on the side of caution, if you are serving a meal that requires specific cutlery, I find that it's safest to offer your guests the standard fork and knife, as well as the specialty cutlery.

To succeed at social and business table etiquette, you must practise skills at home. Once the skills become second nature, you can relax and enjoy yourself in any setting.

TWELVE GOLDEN RULES FOR DINING

Jean Anthelme Brillat-Savarin (1755–1826), a French lawyer and politician, was best known as the author of *La Physiologie du Goût*, or, *Transcendental Gastronomy (The Physiology of Taste)*, published in 1825. In this classic book on gastronomy, the author shares his philosophy on food and dining. Mr. Brillat-Savarin once said, "The discovery of a new dish confers more happiness on humanity than the discovery of a new star." Another of his most famous quotes is this: "Tell me what you eat, and I will tell you who you are."

BUTLER'S TIP
A butter knife is found with the butter dish. Use it to take butter from the butter dish and put it on your side plate. Return this knife to the butter dish and use your butter spreader to dress your bread.

In his chapter "On the Pleasures of the Table,"* M. Brillat-Savarin outlines twelve rules that make for a successful dining experience. These should be part of any etiquette education, and, in fact, are excellent rules to live by. Despite this book being over two hundred years old, its guidelines are timeless.

BRILLAT-SAVARIN'S RULES FOR DINING	MODERN THOUGHTS
1. Let not the number of the company exceed twelve, that the conversation may be constantly general.	Large parties don't allow you time to converse with everyone properly. Keep your guest list intimate, so no one is left out; and your conversation general, so everyone can participate and enjoy the event.
2. Let them be so chosen that their occupations may be varied, their tastes analogous, and that they may have such points of contact that introduction may be useless.	Imagine going to a dinner reception where everyone in the room, including you, does exactly the same job, comes from the same place, and has the same personal background. How boring! But if you invite different kinds of people, what wonderful and varied conversation you will have. Ideally, introduce your guests beforehand to avoid the need for "odious" formal presentations.
3. Let the dining-room be furnished with luxury, the table clean, and the temperature of the room about 16 degrees Celsius.	There is nothing more irritating than dinner in a room that is too hot or freezing cold, too dark or too blindingly lit! The air should be refreshing (not cold), which allows people to eat and drink comfortably (sixteen degrees might be a tad cool for today's standards, but use your discretion); people should be able to see their food to enjoy its visual appeal, but lighting should not be too bright.
4. Let the men be intelligent, but not pedantic— and the women pretty, but not coquettes.	A pompous man or an overly flirtatious woman makes an annoying dinner guest. Relax, be yourself, and don't put on airs!
5. Let the dishes be of exquisite taste, but few in number at the first course; let those of the second be as pleasant and as highly perfumed as possible.	Plain and simple: "Quality over quantity!"

6. Let the order of service be from the more substantial dishes to the lighter, and the simpler wines to the most perfumed.

If you're going to have multiple dishes or wines, start with the softest flavour first, and then move on to the most robust. A strongly flavoured taste will overwhelm and mar everything that comes after it.

7. Let the meal proceed without undue haste, since dinner is the last business of the day; and let the guests consider themselves as travellers about to reach a shared destination together.

Think of a dinner party as a journey. Experience new foods, wines and conversation. The destination should be a memorable and pleasant evening.

8. Let the coffee be hot, and let the master select his own wines.

Hot coffee and quality liquor bring a fine meal to a pleasing end. Don't neglect these important final details.

9. Let the reception-room be large enough to permit those who cannot do without the amusement, to make up a card party, and also for little coteries of conversation.

The room should be large enough that the group can all stay together, yet participate if and as they wish.

10. Let the guests be retained by the pleasures of society, and by the hope that the evening will not pass without some ulterior enjoyment.

May everyone invited enjoy their fellow guests and the way the evening unfolds.

11. The tea should not be too strong, the roast dishes should be loaded artistically, and the punch made carefully.

In other words, attend to the smallest detail!

12. None should begin to retire before eleven o'clock, and at midnight all should have gone to bed.

As a guest, don't leave too early or stay too late. Though not all events will end at eleven, be aware of social cues and read them to know when it's polite to take your leave.

* Brillat-Savarin, Jean Anthelme. *The Physiology of Taste: or, Transcendental Gastronomy.* Trans. Fayette Robinson. Paris: Lindsay & Blakiston, 1854.

HOST AND HOSTESS GIFTS

Personally I find the obsession with host and hostess gifts unnecessary. When I have been a guest at someone's home, I much prefer to wait till after the dinner and send a bouquet of fresh flowers with a handwritten note. The host and hostess might actually have a moment to enjoy them!

Gifts can create a kind of social stress. Should the recipient open them right away? Should flowers be displayed right away? Should the host and hostess serve the wine and chocolates that their guests brought? Should gifts be displayed and announced in front of other guests? Does the host or hostess need to send a thank-you note to guests for their presents (resulting in guests' and hosts' thank-yous crossing paths)? To avoid these conundrums and others, I say, if possible and appropriate, give the gift *after* the party instead of during it, and keep the gift simple. Even a handwritten thank-you note is a lovely way to express gratitude. Also, consider giving the host or hostess a truly memorable gift that will be used over and over again instead of discarded —a copy of this book!

DRESS CODE

When we are dressed appropriately, we feel good about ourselves and we put our best foot forward. And yes, the little black cocktail dress (for women) and the navy suit (for men) are ideal garments to have in your wardrobe.

I remember going for lunch at the York Club in Toronto. I was young and foolish, and I arrived without a dinner jacket. Who knew you had to have a jacket for lunch?

I certainly did not. I was terribly embarrassed. Not only was I barred entry, but also the host who invited me abandoned me at the front door and went in for lunch by himself. I never made that mistake again, and wherever I'm dining, I make sure to have a jacket on hand! Depending on local customs, a country's national dress is also appropriate attire for formal functions.

Invitation Term	Men	Women
WHITE TIE	Black tailcoat, matching trousers with single black stripe of satin or braid in America or two stripes in Europe, white piqué wing-collared shirt with stiff front, white vest, white bow tie, white or grey gloves, black patent shoes and black dress socks.	Formal evening gown
BLACK TIE	Black tuxedo or dinner jacket, white French-cuffed formal shirt, bow tie and cummerbund or vest, white silk or linen handkerchief in the breast pocket (optional), black socks, black patent leather shoes. A white dinner jacket with black trousers is perfectly acceptable in the summer, or on a cruise.	Formal evening dress or cocktail dress.
BLACK TIE OPTIONAL	Many men view this as a welcome opportunity to wear formal attire. A navy blue or black suit with a white French-cuffed dress shirt and an elegant tie is appropriate.	Formal evening dress, cocktail dress or dressy separates.
SEMI-FORMAL	No chance to sport your tuxedo here. The safest bet is to wear a navy blue or black suit with a dress shirt and tie.	Short afternoon or cocktail dress, or a long dressy skirt and blouse or top.
BUSINESS ATTIRE	Even if you normally conduct your business from a home office wearing a dressing gown, this dress code means a suit, dress shirt and tie.	Women's business suit
BUSINESS CASUAL	Slacks with an appropriate sports jacket with open-collar shirt. Business casual is a classic, neat and relaxed look, yet still professional. When in doubt, air on the conservative side.	Reasonable-length day dress, neat and pulled together separates such as skirt or slacks with appropriate blouse or top, pantsuit.

PREPARING TO EAT

When you sit down at any table to "break bread" with family, friends or business associates, there may be a little tension or hesitation before you begin. Perhaps you are thinking, How do I place my napkin on my lap? Can I start the soup or do I need to watch for someone else at the table to begin first? Can I finish my glass of water because I'm really thirsty? What do I do if I need to use the washroom during the meal? What if I absolutely *must* answer my cell phone? No matter what type of table you are at—formal or casual, lunch or dinner—these simple rules may help.

USE YOUR NAPKIN PROPERLY

When you sit down, put your napkin on your lap. The folded seam should face you and the open edges face away from you. When you need to wipe your mouth, do so on the inside of the napkin and then fold it in half again, with the open edge away from you. Why? Because this way, any grease or dirt on the napkin remains hidden from view and it won't stain your clothes.

USE CUTLERY IN THE RIGHT ORDER

No matter where you are in the world, start by using the cutlery farthest from your plate and work your way inwards towards your plate, course by course.

WAIT FOR YOUR HOST OR HOSTESS

Never start your meal before the host or hostess.

BUTLER'S TIP

Young aristocrats in England today have updated the black tie look when dining in private homes. They wear a formal dinner jacket with a dress shirt and an open collar. This fashion shows they know the rules but can break them with confidence and style. Of course, for dining publicly, this attire is often too casual.

WHEN IN DOUBT, WATCH THE HOST OR HOSTESS

Whenever you don't know what to do, never look at the person beside you; instead, look to the host or hostess. It's their table, so they will know what utensils to use with which course.

TAKE PART IN THE CONVERSATION

Although you are there to enjoy your meal—and you should—remember to speak with the diners on either side of you. Don't be afraid to voice an opinion or share a funny and relevant story, provided it is not indiscreet or insensitive.

TOP TEN RULES OF TABLE MANNERS

1. **Your Dinner Napkin:** Never tuck your napkin into your collar. When you want to use your napkin, put your cutlery down first and pick it up from your lap. When you are done with your napkin, place it back on your lap and resume eating.

2. **Elbows:** As your mother always said, no elbows on the table. Also, don't let your elbows stick out at your sides like wings. Keep them tucked into your body, especially when lifting food to your mouth.

3. **When You Don't Like What Is Being Served:** Inevitably there will be times when you don't like the dish being served. Take a little of what is being served, try it, and try not to look unhappy. You don't need to finish it.

BUTLER'S TIP

When seating guests in your home for a formal or official meal, you, as host or hostess, may trump the official list of order of precedence and seat people where you see fit for the betterment of conversation.

4. Bringing Your Fork to Your Mouth: Never lean over the plate. Instead, bring your fork to your mouth.

5. Your Cutlery: Speaking while holding your cutlery and, worse yet, pointing with your cutlery while speaking is considered very rude. And avoid holding your cutlery "as if you are going to war," as my mother always says. Put cutlery down while chewing.

6. Reaching: Never reach for the salt. Ask the person beside you, "Would you pass the salt, please?"

7. Speaking: Never speak with your mouth full. I know, you've heard it before, but it bears repeating.

8. Blowing Your Nose: If you must blow your nose, never do it at the table. Excuse yourself and go to the restroom or elsewhere. Be as quiet as possible so you do not disturb the other guests at the table.

BUTLER'S TIP

If you drop your cutlery at a restaurant or at a formal dinner, leave it on the floor and ask the server to please bring you a new piece. It is considered unhygienic for you to pick it up.

9. Dealing with Spills at the Table: If you accidentally spill something, don't make a big deal about it. If there are servers, motion for one of them to bring you additional napkins. Deal with the problem as quietly and quickly as possible. If you accidentally spill something on someone else, resist the temptation to wipe them down yourself. Instead, offer your napkin.

10. **Concluding Your Meal:** At the end of every meal, the
napkin always goes on top of the table, never on your
chair. Push your chair back into the table; don't leave it
where you got out of it.

HOW TO AVOID PANICKING AT A FORMAL DINNER

Sometimes when people go to formal events or are invited to
a special banquet, they are intimidated by the proceedings. I
understand this reaction; it is normal. And I will admit to
you that over the course of my career, which has included
attending many high-society dinners, occasionally I have felt
intimidated not only by the formality of the table, but by
those seated around it.

Whenever I feel this way, I remind myself that eating
with others is one of the great pleasures of life and of being
human. The table is meant to be enjoyed, first and foremost,
and a meal in an ornate, traditional setting should be no
different—in fact, we should enjoy it even more for the time
and effort that's gone into it. Next, I remind myself that
everyone eats. This is something that unites us all.

Once you are refocused on the great pleasure of dining
and you're feeling calmer about being invited to the table,
that's when it's time to consider etiquette.

A gentleman never sits down until the hostess arrives
at the table; however, once the hostess arrives and invites
everyone to take their seats, a gentleman should assist the
lady to his right with her chair. Then he will seat himself.
Ladies: allow yourself the pleasure of being attended by a

BUTLER'S TIP

In Western culture, burping
in public is considered
embarrassing, but some-
times it's unavoidable. If you
must make such a noise,
do so as quietly as possible
and remember to excuse
yourself afterwards.

gentleman. It's all too rare in today's society for such attention to be paid, so bask in it!

Once you are seated, take your dinner napkin and place it on your lap. A gentleman should then engage in polite conversation with the lady to his right, the same one he helped into her chair. From this point on, everyone can take a deep breath, because no matter what happens, when you don't know what to do, you can just look at the host or hostess. Watch them and follow their lead, take pleasure in the experience of the event, and everything will be just fine.

POLITE TABLE CONVERSATION

"Turning the Table" was once a common term and practice. When a gentleman sat at a dinner table, ideally he was responsible for entertaining the ladies to his right and left. He would start by engaging in polite table conversation with the lady to his right (the one he had helped to seat). Halfway through dinner, he would "turn the table," meaning turn his attention to the lady on his left and converse with her for the remainder of the meal. In today's society, many have lost the art of conversation and our attention spans are short, yet "turning the table" is still a valuable skill. It encourages everyone seated at the table to interact and leads to an enjoyable dinner.

Being able to converse about a variety of subjects is important too. You may be an accomplished lawyer or an expert on hydrangea plants, but that doesn't mean these are topics other people want to hear about. A welcome guest is someone who has knowledge of many topics and shows interest in topics raised by others at the table, in order to carry on a civilized and engaging conversation.

But how do you master the art of conversation? First, make an effort to speak with those on either side of you, and at a normal volume. Yelling at a dinner party will dominate others' conversations—and it's a mark of poor etiquette all around. Second, if you're lost for conversation subjects, say something flattering to your neighbour. Don't gush with false flattery, but find something kind, gracious and sincere to say. Third, come prepared with something to speak about. I recommend reading the newspaper every morning, especially before an important dinner. Alternatively, listen to the news on the radio or on television. Doing so keeps you abreast of current events, and will give you many relevant topics to converse about.

Although being a raconteur is a great skill and a definite asset, be careful what stories you tell, and how you tell them. Make sure they are relevant and appropriate to the listeners. Do you recall the 1958 movie *Auntie Mame*, with Rosalind Russell? Joanna Barnes plays the character Gloria Upson, and while attending an important and upscale social event at her future mother-in-law's home, she attempts to tell a personal story about ping-pong . . . but the story is terribly boring and she fails miserably at winning over the well-heeled crowd. As we watch, we cringe and feel embarrassed for poor Gloria. In many ways, this is a dinner guest's worst nightmare. If there's one piece of advice I'd emphasize here, it is this: When you are a guest, think before you speak!

BUTLER'S TIP

Your mother always told you not to slouch at the table, right? Now I'm telling you too! Sit upright and face forward. At the end of a meal and whenever you get up from the table, push in your chair.

THE BUTLER'S TOOLKIT: THE GUEST BOOK

A guest book provides the host and hostess with a memento in the form of a record of all the guests who have visited their home or attended events there. You often see guest books at castles, palaces, official government residences, stately homes and large country estates. I have always loved these books; it is so much fun to look back at all the people who have visited over the past years. I also believe that guests are honoured to be asked to sign the official guest book of a prominent or important residence.

Here are some tips on using a guest book:

- Purchase an attractive guest book from a traditional stationery supplier.
- Write the name of the occasion and the date at the top of the page. (Entries should be on the right side of the page only.)
- Invite guests to sign the guest book as they leave. (The inviter may be you, as host, or a designated other.)
- Provide guests with a good-quality pen for signing.

HOW TO CORRECTLY HOLD A DINNER KNIFE AND FORK

Knowing how to properly hold and use cutlery is an important aspect of proper table manners. The tips and illustrations that follow will show you how.

Place your forefinger on top of the knife. This gives you more control of the knife when cutting food.

With the tines facing down, hold the fork in a similar fashion as the knife, by placing your forefinger on the fork handle. This will give you more control when you spear the food.

Never hold the fork with a clenched fist. It is not a pitchfork!

DON'T

Never hold your fork by the tip of the handle.
You will not have a firm grip.

DON'T

THE PROPER USE OF CUTLERY DURING THE MEAL

This is the proper presentation for leaving cutlery on your
plate when you have paused during the meal. Make sure the
fork is crossed over the knife with tines facing down.

When pausing, do not leave your cutlery spread out
on the plate. This looks messy.

DON'T

AFTER THE MEAL

When you have finished your meal, place your fork and
knife side by side in the 5-o'clock position.

If you are using only a fork, place the tines up in the
5 o'clock position.

When you have finished your meal do not leave your fork
and knife in this position as it indicates you are not finished.

DON'T

THE BUTTER SPREADER

You may find a butter spreader on your side plate.
After use, put it back exactly as you found it.

EATING STYLES—
HOW TO USE A KNIFE AND FORK

There are two different styles for using your knife and fork when you eat: American and Continental. Both styles are correct.

EATING—AMERICAN STYLE

American-style eating is also called zigzag style because the fork is shifted between the left and right hand through the meal.

When using a fork and knife, the knife is held in the right hand and the fork is held in the left hand, tines facing down. Cut the food one bite-sized piece at a time. Never cut all your food at once. Cut with a slicing motion, never with a sawing motion.

Once you have cut a piece, put the knife down on the edge of the plate with the blade facing in (towards you) and then switch the fork to the other hand to pick up and eat the food.

When you bring the fork to your mouth, keep the tines facing up, never down.

EATING—CONTINENTAL OR EUROPEAN STYLE

In Continental style, you don't shift the fork between your two hands. The knife and fork remain in the same hands throughout the meal.

Once you have cut a bite-sized piece, use the knife to push the food onto the fork, tines facing downward.

The food is speared on the fork, tines facing down, or placed on the back of the fork. Raise the fork with food to your mouth.

HOW TO CORRECTLY USE
A DESSERT FORK AND DESSERT SPOON

At a formal dinner, dessert utensils will be brought out on the dessert plate, with the fork to the left and the spoon to the right. At an informal dinner, the dessert cutlery may be placed on the table above the plate (American style only) or presented on the dessert plate.

Once the dessert plate is placed in front of the diner, the utensils are laid on the table in the same way. Depending on the dessert and the style of dining, dessert may be eaten with either or both utensils.

In the American style of dining, generally either the fork or spoon is used to eat dessert. For more difficult-to-eat desserts, both utensils are used.

In the Continental style of dining, both dessert utensils are used. The spoon is held in the right hand to hold or cut the dessert, while the fork is held in the left hand for eating.

THE DESSERT FORK AND THE DESSERT SPOON AFTER DESSERT

DON'T

When you are finished the dessert, do not leave your dessert fork and dessert spoon in this position as it tells others you are not finished.

DO

When you have finished eating, place your dessert fork and dessert spoon side by side in the 5-o'clock position.

HOW TO CORRECTLY USE A FISH KNIFE AND FORK

The fish course can be a stressful time for some dinner guests. When fish is served whole or as a fillet at a formal dinner, each place setting must be set with a fish knife and a fish fork. Here's how to use these utensils.

Hold the fish knife like a pen, between your thumb and index finger, resting it on the middle finger. Use the knife to flake off a bite-sized portion of fish at a time.

When using the fish knife, hold the fish fork tines down, just as in the Continental style.

If the fish is tender and you are able to eat it with just the fish fork, then hold the fish fork in your right hand, tines up.

Never use the fish knife to cut. Use it to break apart or to flake the fish, or to fillet a whole fish.

DON'T

BUTLER'S TIP

When is it correct to use a fish fork and knife? Only for fish served with bones. If you serve pasta ravioli stuffed with shrimp, you don't need fish cutlery at all because there are no bones.

THE HISTORY OF THE FISH KNIFE AND FORK

MY DEAR FRIEND AND COLLEAGUE Mr. John Robertson taught me everything anyone could ever want to know about fish cutlery. I found this explanation so interesting that I have to share it.

Before the 19th century, fish was traditionally served at the table whole and with bones. It was considered both good manners and practical to eat the fish using two forks. That's why the individual place setting was set for the fish course with two forks, one on each side of the plate. Why two forks and not a knife? Wouldn't it have been harder to eat a whole fish without a knife? How did people cut into the fish? All these questions point to the secret behind how to eat fish correctly: a properly cooked fish doesn't need cutting. It should simply flake away from the bone or the fillet, making a knife unnecessary.

But by the mid-1800s, the middle class was on the rise, and many *nouveau riche* had a desire to spend their *nouveau* money and a yen to show off their newfound status in society. Cutlery manufacturers saw a great opportunity to make more money, so they invented fish cutlery. The well-established aristocratic families turned up their noses at these new implements. Never would they use this newfangled cutlery at *their* tables. Instead, they continued their two-fork tradition as a way of distinguishing themselves. Eventually, however, the style caught on at all tables—old and new—and today, it is customary to use a fish fork and fish knife in polite society.

HOW TO EAT SOUP CORRECTLY—BRITISH STYLE

To fill the soup spoon, start at the edge near yourself and then skim away. Bring the spoon to your mouth and sip from the side of the spoon. Never bring your mouth to the spoon.

When you are almost finished, tilt the soup bowl away from yourself and continue to spoon the soup in the same manner. When you are done, leave the spoon in the bowl, not on the plate underneath.

HOW TO EAT SOUP CORRECTLY—FRENCH STYLE

In French style, dip the soup spoon at the far edge of the bowl and skim the soup towards you. When you are almost finished, tilt your soup bowl towards you, and remember to spoon the soup towards yourself as well.

HOW TO EAT FROM A SOUP CUP CORRECTLY

Soups that are served in soup cups tend to be clear broths and can be sipped directly from the cup, or eaten with a spoon. Thicker soups served in soup cups should always be eaten with a spoon.

When you are served a clear soup in a soup cup, use a bouillon spoon or pick it up by the handles with both hands to drink from. Only drink your soup if the host or hostess does the same. Otherwise, use the spoon, which is the more common method.

HOW TO EAT SOUP CORRECTLY—
JAPANESE STYLE

While many cultures consider slurping and making noise while eating rude, this is not so in Japan. In Japan, the *proper* way to eat noodle soups is to slurp. Use chopsticks to bring the noodles to your mouth, and then slurp them down. Moderate slurping is a sign of appreciation and is considered a compliment to the chef. And there's a practical reason: slurping helps to cool down the noodles, which are served very hot.

Another Japanese custom is to drink soup from the bowl after the solid pieces of food have been eaten with chopsticks. Just like eating from a soup cup, raise the bowl to your mouth with both hands and sip.

Take note that what is proper in Japan does not apply to other Asian cultures. In Thailand, slurping is considered rude.

HOW TO EAT SUSHI

Sushi has become hugely popular in North America over the past twenty years. Even so, many people aren't sure of the correct etiquette. Following are four simple steps that will simplify sushi-eating.

Nigiri sushi (raw fish on rice) is traditionally eaten with your fingers, though today, you will see many people eat it with chopsticks. Some Japanese restaurants offer a wet towel to wipe your hands before eating. If a towel is offered, you are then free to eat it with your hands. Eating nigiri sushi with chopsticks can be difficult since it pinches the bundle and the rice can fall away from the fish.

Pour a small amount of soya sauce in the side dish offered and always dip the sushi fish-side down. Never dip it rice-side down as the rice will absorb too much soya sauce and fall apart. When you put the nigiri sushi in your mouth, place it fish-side down; this is considered the best way to appreciate the taste.

HARD-TO-EAT FOODS

When you're faced with hard-to-eat foods at a social event, don't panic. Take a deep breath and watch your host and hostess. Since they have prepared or approved the menu, they'll know how to eat whatever is being served.

If you have the opportunity, and know you may be eating unusual foods at an upcoming dinner, go to a restaurant with a spouse or friend or even by yourself and try the food—escargots, for example—without any pressure! Practising will increase your confidence.

It may console you to know that even the experts make mistakes. I was once on *The Marilyn Denis Show*, teaching people how to properly eat a stew. I accidentally took too large a bite and couldn't speak because my mouth was full! I got through it by relaxing, and chewing slowly and politely.

Which raises an important point: Never speak with your mouth full. If someone asks you a question, signal with your hand that you're eating and will respond in a second.

APPLES, PEARS, APRICOTS, PLUMS

Never bite into a whole apple or pear at the table. Fresh fruit will be served with a knife and fork. Use the finger bowl to wash your hands before eating fruit. In the American way, cut the fruit into quarters and then remove the core. If you do not like to eat the skin, peel each quarter with the knife. Eat the quarters with your fingers, or cut them into small pieces and eat with the fork. At a formal dinner, always eat fresh fruit with a knife and fork. In the Continental or European style, the fruit is peeled first.

BANANAS

At a formal dinner, bananas are served peeled and whole on the plate. Use your knife to cut the banana into slices, one bite at a time, and eat them with your fork. At informal meals or at the family table, peel the fruit and break off bite-sized pieces with your fingers as you eat.

BERRIES

All berries should be washed, hulled and shaken dry before being served. Traditionally, they are served with cream and fine sugar, and eaten with a spoon. Strawberries may be served unhulled, and are then eaten with your fingers. If sugar is served, put some on your plate. Hold the fruit by the stem or leaves and dip it in the sugar. Eat each berry in one or two bites. Place the stem and leaves on the side of the plate.

MELON *(Honeydew & Cantaloupe)*

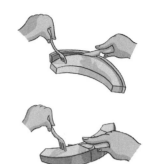

Eat melon that is sliced with the rind removed or cubed with
a fork. Halved melons, melon balls and melon with the rind
still on are eaten with a spoon. Alternatively, use a fork to
hold the fruit while you cut off the rind with the knife. Then
cut and eat a few pieces at a time.

ASPARAGUS

Depending on how the asparagus is prepared, you can eat it
with your fingers or with a fork and knife. Traditionally, it is
eaten with your fingers. If the asparagus is crisp and prepared with sauce on the side, then use your fingers to dip
the flower tip into the sauce. Do not eat the tough woody
ends. If the asparagus is well cooked and covered with sauce,
use a knife and fork.

AVOCADO

Avocado is often served cut in half, with the pit removed
and the centre filled with either vinaigrette or perhaps baby
shrimps in mayonnaise. If the avocado is served in its shell,
lightly hold the avocado skin and use a spoon to scoop out
the filling and the flesh. If the avocado is served peeled and
sliced on your plate (or in a salad), eat it with a fork.

BAKED POTATO

There are several ways to eat a baked potato. Slit the top of the potato lengthwise with your knife. Use your fork to widen the opening and mash some of the flesh with your fork. Season with salt, pepper, sour cream or butter, bacon, chives and any other seasonings. Use your fork to mix in the seasonings as you eat the potato. You may eat the skin; use your knife to cut it into bite-sized pieces. Another way to eat a baked potato is to cut it into slices just as you would a boiled potato. Cut each slice into smaller bite-sized pieces before eating.

CORN ON THE COB

For family and friends gathering for a casual meal, corn on the cob is tasty and fun to eat. Provide miniature prongs to hold the corn. Push one in at each end of the cob. Place some butter on your plate, then butter and season the corn only a few rows at a time. Eat the buttered and seasoned rows slowly and neatly. This is not a race!

BREAD

Watching how a person eats bread can tell you what they know about table etiquette. The proper way is to take a piece of bread or roll from the bread basket and place it on your bread plate or directly on the tablecloth if there is no bread plate. Break off one bite-sized piece at a time with your fingers and butter each piece before you eat it. Do not bite into the bread or roll directly. Always tear a small piece off to

eat. Do not use your knife to cut the bread or. Do not butter the entire piece of bread before eating. The exception to this is toast served at breakfast.

BUTTER

Butter is a condiment, not a food. When there is a shared butter dish at the table, use your butter knife to transfer butter from the dish to your bread plate or dinner plate. Use your butter knife to spread some butter on your bread.

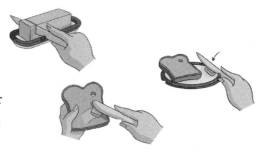

CAVIAR

This expensive delicacy is traditionally served either from the open container in which it was purchased, or transferred to a glass bowl and chilled over ice. Ideally, the caviar should be scooped out with a small mother-of pearl spoon. Alternatively, use a horn, bone or wooden spoon. Never use a metal spoon, as it can imbue the caviar with a harsh metallic taste. Place a teaspoon of caviar on your plate, along with some toast points or blinis, and garnishes of your choice. Assemble one serving at a time. Generally, eat caviar on toast points with your fingers, and caviar on blinis with a knife and fork. Traditional garnishes include grated egg yolks, grated egg whites, finely diced red onion and crème fraîche or sour cream.

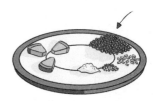

ESCARGOTS

When served out of the shell, escargots are very easy to eat. However, traditionally they are served in the shell, and this presents an etiquette challenge. With a pair of escargot tongs, hold the shell and use the two-pronged escargot fork to pull the meat out. Use the escargot fork to dip escargot into the garlic butter.

BACON

Use a fork and knife to eat cooked bacon. If the bacon is overly crisp, then you have no choice but to use your fingers, but this is a last resort.

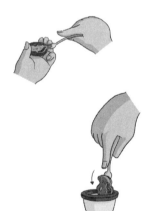

CLAMS

When eating steamed clams, hold the open clamshell in one hand as you remove the meat with a seafood fork. Dip the clam in the clam broth or melted butter, and eat the whole thing in one bite. Place the shell on the side of your plate or in the bowl provided for empty shells. Remember: never eat a clamshell that did not pop open at least halfway in the steaming process. When eating raw clams on the half-shell, hold the shell steady with one hand as you remove the meat with a seafood fork. Dip the clam in the accompanying sauce on your plate, and eat the whole thing in one bite. If the sauce is in a shared dish, spoon it over the clam before removing it from the shell.

SOUP *(Clear)*

Though it may depend on the culture, a clear soup such as a consommé is generally served in a small, round bowl. It may or may not have a lid or handles. The lid will be removed either by the butler or the guest. The proper utensil for eating clear soups is the round soup spoon.

SOUP *(Cream)*

Though it may depend on the culture, a cream or thick soup will be served in a soup plate, which is a wide, shallow bowl with a broad rim. The proper utensil for eating cream or thick soups is the oval-shaped soup spoon.

CONDIMENTS

Never dip your food directly into the shared condiment dish. Condiments will usually be placed on the table with a spoon or knife that stays with the condiment. Once you have served yourself the condiment on your bread and butter plate, or on your main plate, use a small amount at a time on the food you are eating. A condiment is usually added to the food to complement or enhance the flavour. Do not ask for condiments if they are not on the table.

GARNISHES

Garnishes that decorate the plate are not meant to be eaten, even when they are edible.

Part Five

The Art of
Good Housekeeping

IN THE VICTORIAN AND EDWARDIAN eras, cleaning was a matter of pride and decency. Harsh techniques and chemicals were used to clean practically everything in the home. What we have learned today is that cleanliness is possible, even preferable, without the use of toxic chemicals. In fact, harsh techniques and chemicals actually damage the surfaces they touch. A furniture conservator and friend of mine, Mr. Greg Kelly, once described our role in caring for household items as "custodians of fine furniture for future generations." Before he said this, I'd never thought of my butlering role this way. Instead of concentrating on the drudgery and stress of maintaining the cleanliness of every object in a household, I was heartened to think of my role—and indeed the role of all the household staff—as that of a preserver of a kind of legacy. This definitely put the zing back into my polishing cloth.

But no matter how careful we are, when we clean any surface, over time the action of rubbing wears an object down. This is a slow process, to be sure, but it's something to keep in mind. A great example is silver plate. Every time you wash it, you are slowly eroding the tarnish and the silver. Eventually, you rub away the silver and reveal the other metal underneath. Consequently, it's important to clean enough but not too much—though the "enough" will vary from item to item.

Before we go any further, let's define some basic house-keeping terminology.

HOUSEKEEPING

Housekeeping is the day-to-day work that goes into tidying, reorganizing and detailing rooms in a home after it has been properly cleaned. Housekeeping is that extra touch that goes into good presentation. This includes fluffing pillows, positioning furniture correctly, organizing magazines and books, properly making a bed and so on.

Without good housekeeping, a clean room is only a clean room, not necessarily an inviting one. I'm not saying clean is bad—it's simply not enough. A good housekeeper has a fine touch and a keen eye for detail. A clean room can only reach its full potential with good housekeeping.

HOUSE-CLEANING

House-cleaning is the foundational work that goes into keeping a home clean. This includes washing floors, vacuuming carpets, dusting furniture, cleaning shower stalls and toilets, washing bed linens and so on. Remember that a home can be tidy without actually being clean. In many homes, the emphasis is on the surface details that define housekeeping and not on cleanliness. Conversely, a home can also be clean without being tidy. The cleanliness of any living space can be undermined by a lack of organization and attention to the visual presentation. The standard should be a room that's both clean and tidy.

When cleaning a home, take the opportunity to perform preventative maintenance checks. Look for things like leaky faucets, improperly flushing toilets, wobbly door handles and so on. It's always best to address these issues before they become major ones and more costly to repair.

DEEP CLEANING

Deep cleaning is what many households think of as "spring cleaning"; however, for me, deep cleaning includes special projects as well as scheduled cleaning tasks that may or may not correspond with the seasons. Deep-cleaning special projects include polishing silver, vacuuming drapery, cleaning chandeliers, dusting and washing air vents, washing baseboards and so on. Scheduled cleaning events can be coordinated around a season. For example, the seasonal transfer of a wardrobe is the perfect opportunity to wash and clean drawers, closets and shelves.

THE BUTLER'S TOOLKIT: THE CADDY

A good caddy is a time-saving tool. Caddies should have sections that allow you to separate cleaning products and tools. If space is not an issue in your home, you might have different caddies for the kitchen and bathroom, plus a general cleaning caddy for the rest of the home. A good general caddy includes a multipurpose cleaner (such as a vinegar/water solution), an all-purpose pH-neutral soap and water cleaner, non-abrasive cream cleanser, alcohol, baking soda, rubber gloves, clean microfibre cloths, paper towel, sponges, an old toothbrush and a squeegee. Don't forget that the caddy itself needs cleaning every once in a while too.

THE TEN GOLDEN RULES OF HOUSEKEEPING

1. Before you begin cleaning, get your caddy ready.

2. Clean from the least contaminated item in the room
to the most contaminated.

3. Clean a room from top to bottom.

4. A good housekeeper moves his or her eye within a room
from top to bottom, and from left to right.
This helps you to notice details that aren't at eye level.

5. Look at a room from the user's perspective. What will someone
in the room see while sitting down at the table or lying in their bed?

6. Always clean under objects, moving them as necessary.

7. Use cleaning methods that are the least invasive or harmful to surfaces.

8. Dust regularly.

9. Tackle seasonal deep cleans to help reduce the time required
for daily and weekly housekeeping.

10. Don't bother with artificial air fresheners.
A clean home does not require them.

STARTER CLEANING CALENDAR

After years of experience I've devised a simple "starter" calendar that you can use and adapt to suit the needs of your particular household. Use the calendar to ensure that you deep clean one area of your home per month, instead of doing it all at once a couple of times a year. You'll note that there are no tasks scheduled for December—this is a month for you to enjoy entertaining, and spend time with family and friends. While you'll need to do a little house-keeping during the festive season, try not to fuss too much. Enjoy the holidays.

BUTLER'S TIP

A picture frame should be hung with two hooks or nails in the back, not a wire. A wire can easily move or shift and the picture can become crooked.

January
- Deep clean kitchen (post-holiday entertaining)
- Flip mattresses

February
- Clean out all closets
- Deep clean master bedroom

March
- Dust bookshelves
- Deep clean all other bedrooms

April
- Flip mattresses
- Check all outdoor lights for burned-out bulbs
- Deep clean hallways, front hall closet, linen closet

May
- Wash windows
- Clean garage (post-winter mess)
- Deep clean laundry room and basement area

June
- Clean all outdoor barbecue items
- Deep clean outdoor entertaining areas
- Deep clean the kitchen

July
- Flip mattresses
- Deep clean bathrooms

August
- Clean garage (post-summer mess)
- Deep clean kids' rooms; prepare wardrobes for school

September
- Deep clean family room
- Check furnace for winter season

October
- Wash windows
- Flip mattresses

November
- Clean silver (preparing for holiday entertaining)
- Install holiday lights before first snowfall

December
- Enjoy your family and friends!

BUTLER'S TIP

Never spray a cleaning agent directly onto an object—spray your cloth, and then use it to wipe the object. Why? Because that way the spray won't drip and cause a mess for you to clean up later.

HOW TO CLEAN A ROOM

A good rule of thumb when cleaning surfaces in households is to begin with the least invasive cleaning procedure, and work your way through to the most invasive. In other words, it's better to try to clean something first with just a dampened cloth rather than loading your cloth with harsh cleaning chemicals. You can add a more powerful cleaning agent if needed later, but you can't undo damage once an invasive cleaner has been used. And always clean a room from top to bottom (so that any dirt or dust that falls will be picked up) and from left to right (so you can keep track of what you've done).

Step 1: Top to Bottom

Clean from the top of the room to the bottom. Never touch paintings; dust only the frames. Move objects just enough to clean surfaces and surrounding areas. Put things back correctly, symmetrically and with the "housekeeper's eye."

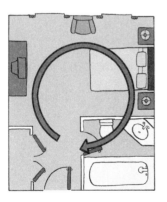

Step 2: Left to Right

Clean from left to the right. In this illustration, cleaning should begin at the doorway, moving to the TV, then around to the bedroom area and, finally, to the bathroom (the least hygienic place in the home).

HOW TO CLEAN A BATHROOM: TEN STEPS

Bathrooms require keen attention. A living room that is not properly kept may appear untidy and dusty, but a bathroom that is not properly cleaned will always create the impression that the home is dirty. Start with the least contaminated area and work your way to the most contaminated.

The following ten steps will help you clean bathrooms efficiently and in the most sanitary way.

Step 1: Dust and clean all surfaces beginning at the top (ceiling, vents and light fixtures), then move on to the walls and all the way down to the baseboards.

Step 2: Dust and clean the windows, windowsills and frames, as well as the window treatments.

Step 3: Fill the bathtub and fully clean it and surrounding elements, like the faucets. Drain it, and then polish the fixtures. Tackle the shower area in the same way. Scrub grout to prevent mildew. Descale showerhead as required.

Step 4: Clean the mirror, soapdish and toothbrush holder (inside and out). Then clean and disinfect sink and vanity counter.

Step 5: Remove all items from the interior and exterior of the vanity, drawers and other storage areas. Clean thoroughly. Reorganize contents and restock as needed.

BUTLER'S TIP

"The Housekeeper's Eye" refers to how a housekeeper appraises a room and addresses every detail. Having "the eye" is both a blessing and a curse—it's wonderful to notice and fix every detail, but you'll never see a room the same way ever again.

Step 6: Clean and disinfect all other bathroom surfaces, such as light switches, doors and doorknobs.

Step 7: Clean and disinfect the toilet and surrounding elements. Always begin by flushing the commode. If there is a bidet, clean the bidet *before* the toilet.

Step 8: Replace bath towels, bath linens and bathroom amenities.

Step 9: Empty the trash bin. Thoroughly clean the interior and exterior.

Step 10: Vacuum or sweep floor thoroughly, removing any area rugs. Then wash and dry the floor using fresh water and a mop.

BUTLER'S TIP

When cleaning your bathroom, use cotton rags instead of paper towels. In addition to being environmentally friendly, it's a great way to re-purpose your old cotton sheets or T-shirts.

TOILET SEAT ETIQUETTE

Keep the toilet seat down and the toilet cover closed.

Even if you have just cleaned the toilet, put the seat down and close the lid.

TOILET PAPER STANDARD

If you've ever stayed in a luxury hotel, you'll have noticed that the housekeeper always leaves toilet paper with a nice fold. This attention to detail gives the guest the impression of cleanliness and care; however, in one's home, this fold may seem ostentatious. Simply make sure that the toilet paper is full (replacing with a fresh roll if necessary), and leave a clean edge.

THE HISTORY OF TOILET PAPER

WE ALL USE IT. And though we don't think about it very often, I know that I, for one, am most grateful for its invention. I suspect you feel the same way.

Paper for the purpose of, ahem, personal hygiene dates back as far as 589AD in China. That's the date of the first known written reference to it. It is commonly known that in the Middle Ages, people used loose straw and leaves, neither of which came conveniently rolled, nor can they have been very pleasant to use. As time progressed, various civilizations took different approaches to improving things. The Romans used a stick with a sponge attached to the end for cleaning and wiping purposes, and by the time Henry the VIII was on the British throne in 1509, royalty and noblemen of the United Kingdom used fancy cloth—linen or cotton—which was, believe it or not, washed by servants and then reused! In America, using pieces of paper from an old Farmers' Almanac was popular, especially because the book had a hole in the top corner so you could hang it on a nail in your outhouse. Once you'd read it . . . well, you get the idea.

It wasn't until the 19th century that toilet paper began to be manufactured in Western civilization. The soft and pliable rolled kind we are familiar with today came into existence in the Edwardian era and was used by those who could afford such luxury—and it *was* considered a luxury at that time. Aren't you grateful that it's now a common item in our homes?

SHOWER CURTAIN ETIQUETTE

There are convincing arguments both ways for whether a shower curtain should be left open or closed. I personally leave mine closed to allow the curtain liner to dry, thus avoiding mould and mildew. More and more hotels, however, are leaving the shower curtain open because guests say they feel safer walking into the bathroom if they can see behind the curtain. But aside from this, an open shower curtain makes a bathroom more inviting and the space feel more open.

For your own home, make a choice that feels best for you and your guests.

If you keep your shower curtain closed, the plastic lining on the other side dries correctly, thus curbing mildew and/or bacteria growth.

This seems to be the more popular look these days. An open curtain makes the bathroom and bathtub more inviting. But check the plastic liner regularly for mould and mildew.

HANGING BATHROOM TOWELS

Hang hand towels "long" (one fold). This looks nicer and cleaner.

When you hang towels "short," they are not as easy to dry your hands on and they don't look as full and luxurious.

CLEANING A BEDROOM: SEVEN STEPS

The bedroom is the area of the house most often neglected when it comes to housekeeping and cleaning. Most of us change our bedsheets regularly, and vacuum frequently, but that seems to be about it. The bedroom collects dust just like every room in your home, so let me ask you this: have you looked under your bed lately? You need to dust, vacuum and deep clean underneath it often. Bedrooms should be clean, odour-free, well organized and properly lit, with beds neatly made. An unmade bed gives the impression of uncleanliness, even if the room is clean.

Follow the steps below to clean a bedroom properly.

Step 1: Put any dirty clothes in the hamper and put away clean clothes.

Step 2: Change linens and remake bed. Inspect blanket or duvet for stains and dry clean as required.

Step 3: Dust and clean all bedroom surfaces and objects, including nightstands, headboards, chairs, lamps, shelves, mirrors, light switches, doors and doorknobs, and telephones.

Step 4: Thoroughly vacuum any upholstered furniture, pillows, cushions and window treatments.

Step 5: Tidy bedroom area so that everything is back in its proper place (e.g., straighten books, put away DVDs).

Step 6: Throw away any garbage and then empty the trash bin.

Step 7: Vacuum area rugs and then remove them to sweep and/or mop the floor.

THE BED

What makes a comfortable bed? I have made beds in luxury hotels and fine homes all around the world, and I'd like to share with you my top three tips for making the perfect bed.

Everyone has their own preferences, of course, but I believe most would agree that the best way to turn a good bed into a great one is to use clean, high-quality sheets! Never use polyester sheets, as they don't breathe and you will sweat when you sleep under them.

After good sheets, the next priority is to use feathers (if you aren't allergic to them!). Not to be confused with a feather duvet, a feather-bed goes on top of the mattress and under the fitted sheet. For me, it makes the bed perfect when you want to crawl inside—it's soft but not too soft, it's fluffy but not too fluffy. And finally, the third thing that makes a great bed is pillows. I like both feather and foam pillows, and love having lots of them around. I don't think you can ever have too many pillows!

HOW TO MAKE A THREE-SHEET BED: ELEVEN STEPS

There are many different styles of bed, but I strongly believe there is only one correct method for making a bed. Pay attention to the details, such as correctly tucking the sheets under the mattress as far as you can to avoid lumps, or making sure you have an equal amount of sheet on all sides. These details will make a difference to you and to your guests. And avoid shortcuts. To correctly make a bed, I strongly believe that you must strip the bed down fully every time.

 **Step 1:** Strip the bed down to the mattress whether you are using new sheets or simply remaking the bed. A stripped bed should always be your starting point.

 **Step 2:** Place the mattress pad protector on the mattress and make sure it is lump free. This is the base of your bed and any imperfections here will become more obvious through the bed-making process.

 **Step 3:** Place the first flat sheet on top of the mattress pad cover. If using a fitted sheet, put it on now and correctly tuck it under the mattress. If using a flat sheet, do not tuck the sheet under the mattress. Let it hang evenly on all sides.

Step 4: Align the second flat sheet (or first one, if you've used a fitted sheet in the previous step) exactly on top of the first sheet.

Step 5: Align the blanket exactly on top of the second sheet.

Step 6: Align a third and final sheet exactly on top of the blanket.

Step 7: Tuck the sheets and blanket well under the mattress at the foot of the bed.

Step 8: Move to the top of the bed, pull the sheets taut, and turn the second sheet over the blanket and third sheet to create a neat edge.

Step 9: Moving back down the bed, create "hospital corners." To do this, pinch the sheet that is hanging over the foot of the bed and draw up all the material into one hand so that the hanging material forms a triangle. Fold and tuck the excess material under the length of the bed just as you would if you were wrapping a present. Finally, tuck the triangle of bedding under as well to create a neat corner.

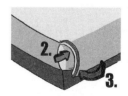

Step 10: Tuck in the sides, nice and tight.

Step 11: Once all the sheets are neatly tucked in, place the bedspread on top of the bed, and finally the pillows.

CLEANING FLOORS

The days of cleaning any floor with a mop and a big pail of water filled with soap are long gone. Why? First, because floor surfaces have changed, demanding new cleaning methods; and second, because technology has changed. We have learned that more water and more soap do not necessarily make floors cleaner. In fact, too much water damages the floor. And remember that whatever amount of water and soap you put on the floor, you're going to have to mop it back up into the pail! Using just enough actually makes cleaning easier.

We've also seen an improvement in the tools we use. I've noticed a shift to microfibre mops, which are more effective than traditional cloth mops at catching stray dust or hairs that may have been missed during sweeping.

The floor should be the last part of a room cleaned (remember the top-to-bottom rule mentioned earlier). Follow these steps to make your floors shine.

Step 1: Remove all objects from the floor.

Step 2: Sweep the entire floor to remove any loose debris prior to washing. Once the floor is wet, it will be difficult and possibly dangerous to remove dirt and debris, as you could slip and fall.

Step 3: Fill the mop bucket with a cleaning solution of pH-neutral soap and hot water (1 capful of soap to 1 gallon of water).

Step 4: Check that there is no debris in the microfibre mop head that might scratch the floor, place the mop in the bucket and let it absorb the cleaning solution.

Step 5: Wring the excess liquid from the mop. The mop head should be damp, not soggy.

Step 6: Begin mopping from the farthest corner of the room, moving towards the exit.

Step 7: Dip and wring out the mop periodically as you work. You may have to change the mopping water if it becomes dirty or cools off.

Step 8: Remember to mop behind the doors. Closing doors before you start will remind you to mop these areas.

Step 9: Repeat this process using fresh water to rinse off the cleaning solution. Once again, make sure that your mop is damp only.

DRYING FLOORS

Once the floor is washed and rinsed, dry it immediately. There are two ways to dry the floor: going over it with a clean, dry mop, or wiping it with a clean dry cloth while on your hands and knees. Never leave a wet floor to air dry.

MOP DRYING A FLOOR

Step 1: Dry the open areas of the floor with a clean, dry mop starting from the farthest corner of the room, moving towards the exit.

Step 2: If you are using a clean, dry, string-head mop, place the mop head flat on the floor and keep it on the floor while swishing it continuously from left to right.

Step 3: Continue moving the mop from side to side as you step backwards, working your way towards the exit.

Step 4: Dry baseboards and other hard-to-reach places with a clean cloth.

Step 5: Repeat this drying process twice.

HAND DRYING FLOORS

Step 1: Equip yourself with several clean, dry cloths. I recommend wearing kneepads for protection on hard surfaces.

Step 2: On your hands and knees, starting from the farthest corner of the room and moving towards the exit, wipe the floor dry.

Step 3: Change the drying cloth as required.

Step 4: Remember to dry baseboards and hard-to-reach places.

CARING FOR SPECIFIC FLOORING TYPES

CERAMIC FLOOR

Step 1: Most ceramic floors are sealed. In this case, vacuum the floor using the soft-brush attachment, then wash it with warm water only.

Step 2: Dry the floor as you go. If the floor still has any sticky residue, remove this with a solution of warm water and a pH-neutral detergent. Dry it again.

A cork floor provides a very resilient surface; however, it requires different care from other wood floors. Standing water will definitely stain a cork floor so use water sparingly.

Step 1: Vacuum the floor using the soft-brush attachment.

Step 2: With a well-wrung mop that is damp only with a solution of a pH-neutral detergent and warm water, begin washing the floor.

Step 3: Dry as you go.

HARDWOOD FLOOR

Step 1: Make sure that any furniture placed on hardwood floors has protector pads.

Step 2: Use area rugs for high-traffic areas to minimize wear and tear on the floor.

Step 3: Vacuum rugs or area rugs.

Step 4: Vacuum the floor's wood surface using the soft-brush attachment.

Step 5: Wet mop only, and never flood a wood floor with water. The best procedure is to clean small areas at a time. Wet mop and dry one area before moving on to the next.

Step 6: While cleaning, if you notice anything unusual about the wood floor surface (stains, cracks, buckling, etc.), address it right away. Check the humidity level in your home. The ideal humidity for most wood floors is between 40 and 50 percent.

LAMINATE FLOOR

Most laminate floors today are highly resilient. Vacuuming them with a soft brush attachment and mopping with warm water should be sufficient. Do one small area at a time, mopping and then drying it before moving on to the next.

MARBLE OR STONE FLOOR

Marble is a very soft stone and is easily damaged. Maximum care is required when cleaning.

Step 1: With the softest brush attachment, vacuum the floor.

Step 2: Make sure the mop head is free of debris. (This is particularly important when cleaning marble floors.)

Step 3: Mop the floor with water only. Work on one small area at a time and dry it before moving on to the next.

Step 4: If there is sticky debris on the surface and wet mopping is insufficient, use a solution of warm water and pH-neutral detergent.

BUTLER'S TIP

Never drag furniture across the floor. Work in teams to move furniture safely and to avoid causing damage.

DUSTING AND VACUUMING

Dusting and vacuuming on a regular basis is important because built-up dust will only attract more dust. Damp dusting is by far the best method, but when cleaning with water, don't use too much of it. Aim for less rather than more. See the illustrations and instructions below.

One of the teachers at my academy, Mr. Greg Kelley, taught me a wonderful dusting tip. Mr. Kelley uses this technique while cleaning museums and clients' homes. He recommends using 100 percent cotton dusting cloths, as anything with polyester will not absorb water well. Old bedsheets that have been cut up into squares are perfect for this task.

Some people ask me about dusting polishes, but I'm not a fan. I believe they're bad for your furniture because of the silicone in many of them. It builds up over time and actually attracts more dust.

Ultimately, the dusting technique below, if done regularly, is all you will ever need.

Step 1: Put your hands under cool or warm running water.

Step 2: Dry your hands with your dusting cloth. Now this cloth has the perfect amount of humidity to dust almost any object without damaging it; no chemicals are needed.

VACUUMING

There are many different types of vacuum cleaners and each has its purpose. It is important to purchase and use the right vacuum cleaner for your space. The most important element is suction, and I recommend vacuums that offer both high and low suction capability.

Here are some tips to remember:

- Dust and vacuum using the top-to-bottom principle. If you vacuum from the floor to the ceiling, you might wind up with dust or dirt falling back onto your already-cleaned floor.
- Change the vacuum cleaner bag before it becomes full. The vacuum becomes less efficient once the bag is close to full, and the trapped debris can harm the motor.
- Vacuum once a week or more often in high-traffic areas.

HEAVY-DUTY RUGS

In general, clean carpets and floors last in a room. Vacuum area rugs before vacuuming the floor. To do this, shake all loose debris from the rug(s). Sweep up debris, using a dustpan or vacuum to pick it up. Then, vacuum the area rug, starting at the point farthest from the exit. Use the crevice vacuum tool to vacuum between a wall-to-wall carpet and the baseboard.

DELICATE RUGS AND FABRICS

The more suction a vacuum has, the greater the risk of damaging the item being vacuumed. A very strong vacuum might pull on the loose ends of a rug, for instance, and tear delicate fibres. To avoid this, when vacuuming delicate fabric surfaces such as upholstery, place a piece of nylon monofilament over the nozzle of the flat upholstery tool.

CREATING THE PERFECT GUEST BEDROOM

The comfort and style of the guest bedroom is part of your visitor's overall experience and should reflect that of the rest of the house. You want your guest to be able to relax there and get a good night's sleep.

A word of advice: I learned from a former employer that sleeping in a guest bedroom yourself for one or two nights is the best way to notice the little details that can be improved. You can't imagine the things I have noticed by doing this.

Provide the following to create the perfect guest bedroom:

- Extra blankets and pillows
- At least one electrical outlet for cell phones and computer chargers
- An alarm clock
- A phone

- Notepaper, a pen and sharp pencils beside the phone or in another convenient spot in the room
- Internet access
- A good reading light beside the bed
- A radio and/or television
- Light reading material handy (magazines or favourite books) and/or playing cards

BUTLER'S TIP

A good butler knows how to improvise when disaster strikes. Whether it's a needle and thread, double-sided tape or duct tape, a butler will always have something on hand to deal with any emergency.

KITCHENS

A kitchen should be functional, which means attention should be paid to every housekeeping detail, but it also serves as a gathering place for the family. It should therefore be clean and organized, but also comfortable.

Think about your lifestyle when you shop for products: Do you love to bake? Would a gourmet stand mixer be useful, brighten up your kitchen and give you enjoyment? When I was growing up, my parents belonged to a gourmet cooking club, so they had all sorts of specialized appliances— like a pot in which you could poach a whole fish. However, people who don't enjoying cooking don't need such supplementary items. The important thing is that you create the kitchen atmosphere you want, while staying within your budget.

From a hygiene perspective, the kitchen must be kept clean or else the food prepared in it may become contaminated and cause illness.

Follow these steps to keep your kitchen spotlessly clean.

Step 1: Stock your cleaning caddy with the required tools and cleaning products.

Step 2: Clean and disinfect kitchen surfaces, including counters, cabinet and door handles, and backsplashes.

Step 3: Clean and disinfect the sink and stopper.

Step 4: Wipe down appliances and other kitchen articles, such as the stovetop, oven, range hood, refrigerator, microwave, toaster, coffeemaker, dish rack. Where possible, clean the inside of the appliance, too.

Step 5: Clean all other kitchen surfaces such as kitchen table, chairs, light switches, doors, doorknobs, telephone.

Step 6: Empty, clean and disinfect the interior and exterior of the trash bin.

Step 7: Sweep, mop and dry the floor.

IRONING A SHIRT

Check the care label for the proper ironing instructions and temperature settings. Always lightly dampen cotton and linen shirts with water using a spray bottle before ironing.

Step 1: Spread the collar out on the ironing board with the underside facing up. Iron the underside first and then turn it over and iron the outside. Use the tip of the iron, pressing from the collar points and working towards the middle.

Step 2: Iron the front yoke, starting with the shoulder areas first, and then the back yoke.

Step 3: Use a spray bottle with water to keep the shirt damp. Iron the cuffs by pressing the inside of the cuff first, then the outside.

Step 4: Lay the sleeve flat on the ironing board, with the cuff opening up, and begin ironing from the shoulder seam down to the cuff. Turn the sleeve over to iron the other side. Repeat the process with the other sleeve.

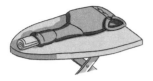

Step 5: For finer shirts and blouses, roll the sleeves, rather than ironing them flat and creasing them. To do this, use a sleeve board or place a tightly rolled towel in the sleeve.

Step 6: Iron the body of the shirt starting with one front panel, then the corresponding back panel. Then iron the remaining front panel and corresponding back panel.

Step 7: Use the tip of the iron to press the area around buttons. Never iron over the buttons.

Step 8: When you are finished ironing, hang the shirt on a hanger and fasten the top button.

BUTLER'S TIP

When ironing a shirt, don't iron a crease into the sleeve. There should not be a seam running down your sleeve—though you may see one when a shirt comes back from the dry cleaner.

IRONING TEMPERATURE CHART

Fabric	Temperature Setting
Cotton	Always use high heat when ironing cotton, and for best results, use the steam function. For cotton dress shirts, never iron a crease into the sleeve. Use a sleeve board or a rolled towel (see page 206).
Denim	Denim is a thick fabric so the heat takes longer to permeate. High heat and plenty of steam are a must.
Lace	Iron on a low to medium heat. Always cover the lace with a damp cotton cloth, then press. Don't use the steam function.
Linen	Linen is hard to iron. Always use high heat and full steam. Spraying the garment with a water bottle will help remove wrinkles.
Nylon	Ideally, nylon should not be ironed, but if it's required, use a low heat setting and iron on the reverse side of the garment.
Polyester	Polyester is ideally steamed, not ironed. But, if ironing, use a press cloth and set on low to medium heat.
Satin	Use a low heat, and never use steam, as it tends to leave water marks on the fabric. Use a slightly damp press cloth and start ironing on the reverse side of the garment. If necessary, touch-up any wrinkles on the front side.
Silk	The same directions apply here as for satin. Use low heat and no steam. The moisture from the press cloth is sufficient.
Trims, Beads & Accents	Never iron!

BUTLER'S TIP

Always follow the fabric chart on your iron's temperature selector or instructions in the owner's manual.

But even with the proper temperature setting, some fabrics will need the protection of a press cloth.

LAUNDRY SYMBOLS CHART—IRONING

Care Symbol	Written Care Instructions	What the Care Symbol and Instructions Mean
	Iron, Any Temperature, Steam or Dry	Regular ironing may be needed, and may be performed at any available temperature. Using steam is acceptable.
	Iron, Low	Regular ironing, steam or dry, may be performed at a low setting (110 degrees C; 230 degrees F).
	Iron, Medium	Regular ironing, steam or dry, may be performed at a medium setting (150 degrees C; 300 degrees F).
	Iron, High	Regular ironing, steam or dry, may be performed at a high setting (200 degrees C; 290 degrees F).
	Do Not Steam	Steam ironing will harm the garment, but regular dry ironing at the indicated temperature setting is acceptable.
	Do Not Iron.	Item may not be smoothed or finished with an iron.

TYPES OF HANGERS

There is no such thing as "one hanger fits all."

Always hang clothing on the most appropriate hanger to extend the life of the garment. And when you have ironed and hung your clothes, try not to crowd them in your closet—which will just lead to your having to re-iron them later. Give your clothes some breathing room and you'll only have to iron once.

The following are the most common types of hangers.

BUTLER'S TIP

Pants hangers are great
for travelling because they
are so lightweight.

MAN'S SUIT HANGER

A large, contoured wooden hanger for suit jackets.
The hanger will have either a bar over which to drape
the suit pants or a pant clip that allows you to hang pants
from the cuffs.

MEN'S OR LADIES' SUIT HANGER

A contoured hanger with clips to hang suit pants or a skirt.

SHIRT / BLOUSE HANGER

This is a solid wooden hanger suitable for hanging men's
shirts or ladies' blouses.

PANTS HANGER

A well-made pant hanger should have felt between the wood
slats, to prevent the pants from falling out.

PANTS OR SKIRT HANGER

This is great for both men's and ladies' garments.

METAL PANTS HANGER

A great metal pants hanger, especially useful in closets where space is limited, this is ideal for hanging pants on a low rod in the closet.

PADDED HANGER

Satin padded hangers are designed for hanging women's delicate garments.

HOW TO SEW ON A FOUR-HOLE FLAT BUTTON

Everyone should know how to sew on a button. It's a must-have skill that can come in handy in an emergency. There are a million wrong ways to sew on a button. These will result in odd puckering, or worse, the button popping right off again. Best to do it properly the first time.

Step 1: Pick a thread to match the button or fabric and cut off about 18 to 20 inches of thread. Thread your needle, then even up the two ends and knot them together so that you have a double strand.

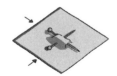

Step 2: Mark position of button with two silk pins as shown.

Step 3: Turn the fabric over to the underside and insert the needle in a corner close to the intersecting point of the two pins.

Step 4: Turn the fabric so the right side is facing up. Lay the button in position on top of the pins. Pull the needle up through the fabric and the nearest hole.

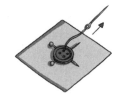

Step 5: Bring the needle down through the closest button-hole and through fabric. Make three or four more stitches to secure this pair of holes.

Step 6: Repeat the process with the next pair of holes.

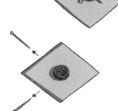

Step 7: Remove the pins.

Step 8: Pull the needle out between the button and fabric. Lift the button so the thread is taut.

Step 9: Wind the thread tightly under the button several times to create a shank. This will make the button stand up on its own.

Step 10: Pull the needle down through the fabric to the wrong side.

Step 11: Make a stitch under the button stitches but instead of pulling it tight, loop the needle back through the hole to make a knot.

Step 12: Cut the thread as close to the knot as possible.

THE BUTLER'S TOOLKIT: EMERGENCY SEWING REPAIR KIT

Whether you're dealing with a wardrobe malfunction, a torn hem or a loose thread, I can't stress this enough—a good sewing kit can save the day. It should include a combination of straight pins and silk pins (for delicate or lightweight fabrics). As well, you'll want double-sided tape, threads in a variety of basic colours (black, white and navy), measuring tape, safety pins, a small pair of scissors and a lint brush.

BUTLER'S TIP

Oh, the wonders of duct tape. Though it may look unseemly, it really does work miracles! If you find yourself with a torn hem and no sewing kit, a little piece of duct tape can provide a temporary fix. Just be sure to properly repair your hem after the event.

BUTLER'S TIP

If you pack a T-shirt for travel and don't want it to wrinkle, lay a sheet of tissue paper on the shirt as you fold it. When you unpack, remove the tissue paper, and the shirt will be far less wrinkled!

FOLDING

There's a right way and wrong way to fold every clothing item. Folding the right way results in fewer wrinkles and means clothes are always ready to wear without the additional work of ironing.

FOLDING A T-SHIRT

Step 1: Lay the garment on a flat work surface, facing down.

Step 2: Fold in both sides a quarter of the way, then fold down the short sleeves.

Step 3: Fold up the bottom of the garment a third of the way.

Step 4: Fold the bottom up again until it reaches the top.

HOW TO FOLD A DRESS SHIRT

Step 1: Lay the garment on a flat work surface, facing down.

Step 2: Fold one arm over the back of the garment, then bring it downward.

Step 3: Repeat the same action with the second sleeve.

Step 4: Fold up the bottom part of the garment a third of the way.

Step 5: Fold the bottom up again until it reaches the top.

BUTLER'S TIP

Anytime you have an item that comes stored in plastic—such as a shirt
from the dry cleaners—remove the plastic immediately so that the fabric
can breathe. Otherwise, the fibres will break down and the
fabric will turn yellow—and that stain will never come out.

HOW TO FOLD PANTS

Step 1: If possible, hang pants from the bottom; this allows the fabric to breathe and allows the wrinkles to fall out.

Step 2: If space is a problem, the next best thing is to hang pants folded in half.

Step 3: When all else is not possible, folding pants into three and putting them in a drawer is the best option.

HOW TO FOLD SOCKS

Step 1: Lay the socks on a flat work surface.

Step 2: Begin rolling from the closed section to the rim (open) section of the socks.

BUTLER'S TIP

Pants: Always hang pants from the cuffs. The weight of the pants will pull out any wrinkles.

Socks: Never fold over the rim or cuff of the socks. This distorts their shape, and the cuffs will lose their elasticity.

CLEANING AND POLISHING SHOES

You can tell a lot about someone by the state of their shoes. It's important to know how to care for your footwear and keep it looking its best. Polishing shoes is straightforward, but it can go terribly wrong very quickly if you're not doing it right.

The most common problem is using the wrong shoe polish, for instance using black shoe polish on dark navy shoes. If you don't have the right colour, use clear polish.

Before beginning the task, assemble everything you need—clean rags and buffing cloths, the right colour of shoe polish and a horsehair brush. Always work on a clean, flat surface covered with an old cloth or towel.

Here is the proper method for cleaning shoes.

Step 1: Always remove the shoelaces first. This allows you to polish the shoe tongue properly and prevents polish from staining the laces. Make note of how the shoes were laced in order to re-lace them the same way.

BUTLER'S TIP

For some unknown reason, women's shoes don't seem to need polishing as often as men's. You may find they need to be cleaned, but they usually maintain their shine quite well and tend to wear better over time.

BUTLER'S TIP

Never put freshly polished shoes back in a wardrobe or closet. Instead, place them outside or in a well-ventilated room for a couple of hours so the smell of the polish doesn't permeate the rest of your wardrobe.

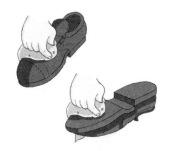

Step 2: Wipe down the shoe with a damp (not wet) cloth to remove any dirt. Clean the bottom of the shoe to remove dirt, dried gum or any other debris that has stuck to the sole.

Step 3: With a different cloth, apply the shoe polish lightly and evenly to the leather parts of the shoe. Work in a circular motion to massage the polish into the leather. Never apply shoe polish to the bottom of the shoe.

Step 4: Once the polish has dried, buff with a horsehair brush using a back-and-forth motion. You should always buff in the same direction for both shoes. Buff until the shoe shines.

Step 5: Rub the shoe with a dampened buffing cloth. This will give the shoe an extra shine.

Step 6: Re-lace the shoes.

HOW TO FOLD A SHEET

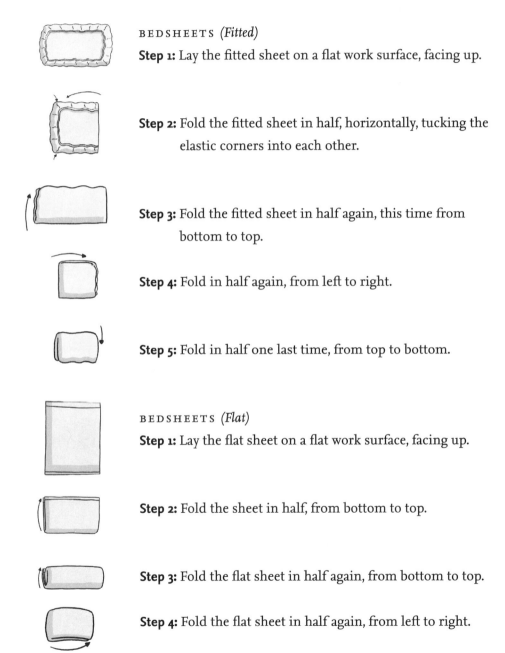

BEDSHEETS *(Fitted)*

Step 1: Lay the fitted sheet on a flat work surface, facing up.

Step 2: Fold the fitted sheet in half, horizontally, tucking the elastic corners into each other.

Step 3: Fold the fitted sheet in half again, this time from bottom to top.

Step 4: Fold in half again, from left to right.

Step 5: Fold in half one last time, from top to bottom.

BEDSHEETS *(Flat)*

Step 1: Lay the flat sheet on a flat work surface, facing up.

Step 2: Fold the sheet in half, from bottom to top.

Step 3: Fold the flat sheet in half again, from bottom to top.

Step 4: Fold the flat sheet in half again, from left to right.

Step 5: Fold the flat sheet in half one last time, from the left to right.

PILLOWCASES

Step 1: Lay the flat pillowcase on a flat work surface, facing up.

Step 2: Fold the pillowcase a quarter of the way in from the left and a quarter of the way in from the right.

Step 3: Fold the pillowcase in half from right to left.

Step 4: Fold the pillowcase in half again, from bottom to top.

Step 5: Fold the pillowcase in half one last time, from bottom to top.

BUTLER'S TIP

If you organize your bedrooms so that everyone has similar coloured sheets—white, for example—they are much easier to organize. You can mix and match based on texture, and if one sheet wears out, you can easily substitute another.

FOLDING AND CARING FOR TABLECLOTHS

Tablecloths need to be washed immediately after use and stored in a clean place. When setting your table, place an underpad beneath the tablecloth—this will give your table a soft, cushiony look, and protect the table from heating damage.

HANGING OR ROLLING

The advantage of hanging a tablecloth, if you have the space, is to keep wrinkles from forming. Rolling it is also effective for this reason. The fewer creases there are in your tablecloth, the better. That said, don't ever iron one directly on the table!

FOLDING

And if you must fold a tablecloth for storage, ensure that the creases run lengthwise.

FOLDING A SQUARE OR RECTANGULAR TABLECLOTH

Step 1: Lay the tablecloth on a flat work surface, facing up.

Step 2: Fold the tablecloth in half, from right to left.

Step 3: Fold the tablecloth in half again, from right to left.

Step 4: Fold the tablecloth in half again, from top to bottom.

Step 5: Finally, fold the tablecloth over a padded hanger.

FOLDING A ROUND OR OVAL TABLECLOTH

Step 1: Lay the tablecloth on a flat work surface, facing up.

Step 2: Fold the tablecloth in half, from bottom to top.

Step 3: Fold the tablecloth in half again, from top to bottom.

Step 4: Fold the tablecloth in half again, from right to left.

Step 5: Fold the tablecloth in half again, from left to right.

Step 6: Only if necessary, fold the tablecloth in half one more time, from left to right.

BUTLER'S TIP

Dryer sheets can harm your clothes dryer because they leach chemicals that coat your dryer vent. Using them with tablecloths, however, helps to repel liquid, like spilled red wine. Never use dryer sheets when drying bath towels: it reduces their absorbency.

Before you go . . .

GLOSSARY

24-Inch Rule

The ideal amount of space from the centre of one plate to the centre of the plate beside it when setting a rectangular table. Also, the backs of all chairs at a table ideally should be 24 inches from the table's edge.

Afternoon Tea

The British tradition of late-afternoon tea served along with miniature sandwiches, scones with strawberry jam and small pastries.

Butler

Originally a man who worked within the household who held the key to the wine cellar and made the beer. In the
mid 19th century and the early 20th century this became a service role. The butler served the meals and beverages, and answered the door. This role has also been described as *chief manservant of the house.*

Butler's Book

This traditional book was updated and managed by butlers and kept in the butler's pantry. This book kept all the household inventories and family information that allowed the butler to do his job properly. This book is also called the *Pantry Book* and today, the *Household Procedures Manual.*

Chamber Maid

The chamber maid cleans and maintains the private bedrooms of the household. In the past, this job was especially difficult, as chamber maids were required to carry many buckets of water up and down the stairs for their employers' baths.

Charger or Charger Plate

A large plate placed under the dinner plate used with some formal table settings. The charger is traditionally bigger than any other plate used during that meal. The charger is already on the table when guests sit down and is only removed with the main course dinner plate. In some households the charger remains until after dessert has been eaten.

Chef

A man or woman who runs and manages the kitchen as the head of that department.

Deep Cleaning

Deep cleaning is sometimes known as *spring cleaning*, but it should be done throughout the year. It includes special projects, such as cleaning chandeliers.

Estate Manager

An estate manager manages one large estate or, in some cases, multiple estates for one employer. This is traditionally a desk job and one that does not involve service.

Finishing School

Originating in Switzerland, this type of private school for girls focuses primarily on etiquette and culture. Traditionally, finishing school was followed by a post-secondary education. Today, the few remaining finishing schools are still found in Switzerland. The oldest remaining school is the Institut Villa Pierrefeu.

First Footman

A servant employed in a large residence whose job it was to run errands, do chores, attend to the door and wait table. The first footman reported directly to the butler, and was often in training to become a butler himself.

French Polishing

A wood finishing technique (and not a substance, as commonly assumed) that results in a very high gloss, deep colour and tough surface. Many thin coats of shellac are applied with a cotton pad. This technique of applying shellac came into widespread use in the 19th century.

Gentleman's Gentleman

A manservant who takes care of a single gentleman. This person is responsible for all aspects of the gentleman's life, including cooking, running errands, seeing to his clothing, supervising trades and supervising a cleaning person and/or housekeeper. Generally once the man gets married the gentleman's gentleman leaves to work for another single gentleman, and the married man hires a butler.

Governess

A well-educated woman who lives with the family and educates and helps to raise the children. These days only royal households and a few high-end residences hire governesses. Governesses were usually from upper-middle-class families but not part of the aristocracy; however, because they lived with the family and because of their education, they did not entirely fit in among the servants. This often left them feeling isolated.

House Cleaning

The foundational work that goes into keeping a home clean. It includes washing floors, vacuuming carpets, dusting furniture, cleaning shower stalls and toilets, washing bed linen and so on.

Household Manager

The American term for butler is *household manager*. This position involves less daily service than that of a butler. It is more of a desk job and entails managing the affairs of the residence, the family and other household employees.

Household Procedures Manual

This is the modern-day version of the Butler's Book. The butler and or household manager keep the *Household Procedures Manual*. This book is used only by the butler /household manager.

Housekeeper

Traditionally this title was given to the highest-ranking female servant in a household. The housekeeper was responsible for selecting and managing female staff,
managing household accounts, procuring goods and managing internal stores and household linen. In most homes today, this role is filled by the *executive housekeeper*. Some traditional homes, however, still have a housekeeper as the head of domestic staff.

Housekeeper's Eye

This refers to detailing, which goes beyond cleaning and means making a room look good. This includes adjusting lighting, fluffing pillows, arranging curtains, putting the remote control in its proper spot and so on.

Housekeeping
The day-to-day work that goes into the tidying, reorganizing and detailing of a room after it has been properly cleaned.

Kitchen Maid
Traditionally, this maid was responsible for keeping the kitchen clean for the chef and sous chef. The kitchen maid lit the fires, kept the stove and oven burning, cleaned vegetables, peeled potatoes and performed all kinds of food preparation.

Lady's Maid
This was the lady's servant who took care of a married woman at home. She was responsible for the clothing, alterations and dressing of the lady of the house. She would travel with the lady as required. She worked directly with the valet. This position is rare today.

Land Steward
The land steward was a highly educated gentleman whose job was to manage the estate profitably. He was usually the highest-paid employee of the estate.

Maid
This was a full-time position, generally held by a woman whose duties were to clean and report to the housekeeper. Today, the term *maid* is rarely used and the role has been replaced by that of the housekeeper, who reports to an executive housekeeper.

Major-Domo
This is an old Latin word for *master of the house*. The term *major-domo* is not often used anymore, but I happen to love it. The major-domo was responsible for the entire household, as butlers are.

Military Service
Sometimes called *ballet of service*, this is an American term used to describe a particular style of table service. The waiters circle the table, and each waiter stands behind one female guest. At the head waiter's signal, each woman around the table is served at the same time. The process is repeated for the gentlemen guests as well. All the waiters leave the room together, in the same order as they entered it.

Nanny

People often say, "I have a nanny for my children," when what they really have is a babysitter. A nanny does not just watch over the children but is supposed to stimulate and teach children outside the school curriculum.

Parlour Maid

This maid would dust and sweep the drawing room, dining room, front hall and sitting room, as well as light fires in each place. The parlour maid would never speak to the master or mistress of the house unless spoken to first, and if anyone entered the room she was cleaning, she would discreetly slip out.

Percale Cotton

Percale refers to how a material is woven. A percale bedsheet, for example, could be 50 percent cotton and 50 percent polyester, but still qualify as percale if it uses the tightly woven finish that results in an extra-smooth fabric.

Personal Assistant

Generally the person in the household who reports directly to either the master or mistress and takes care of all personal and private matters.

Safe Room

Also called the *panic room*, the safe room was a place considered to be safe from outside intrusions. Food and supplies were kept inside, in case the family needed to spend a few days in the room to be safe from danger or natural disasters.

Scullery Maid

Considered the lowest position for a female within an estate. Scullery maids washed dishes, often for hours at a time and using toxic chemicals.

Second Footman/Basic Footman

The second footman reported to the first footman, and was also in training to continue up the domestic service ladder. A basic footman was the male entry-level position in the world of service.

Social Secretary

This position is rare these days and found only in royal households, embassies and old-money homes. The social secretary is responsible for all social correspondence and protocol for events at the residence as well as all social invitations and RSVPs outside of the home, etc.

Sous Chef

Works in the kitchen under the direction of the chef. The sous chef in a large kitchen would be the second in command of the kitchen brigade.

Surface Cleaning

This refers to tidying up a room quickly, not deeply. It could involve wiping down a counter, putting away dirty dishes or picking up dirty laundry.

Underbutler

A service person who works in the household under the butler. The underbutler is in training to one day be a butler. There can be several underbutlers in one home.

Valet

This servant took care of a married man at home, seeing to his clothing and personal errands. Generally he was not responsible for any service within the household, but might assist in a pinch. He would travel with the master and work directly with the lady's maid. This position is rarely seen today.

FOOD AND WINE PAIRINGS

Artichokes	Loire Sauvignon Blanc	Cheese	
		Brie	Beaujolais
Asparagus	Pinot Gris		Alsace Pinot Noir
	Good Chardonnay		
	Young Muscat d'Alsace	*Camembert*	Southern French Red like
	Medium-Bodied White		Corbières or Fitou
Burgundy			
		Cheddar	Light Claret
Avocado	Champagne		New Zealand Sauvignon Blanc
	Chablis		
	Alsace Gewürztraminer	*Chèvre*	Muscadet
			Sancerre
Barbecues	Well-chilled, crisp white		
	Lightly chilled, young and	*Emmental*	Light Cru Beaujolais
	fruity reds		California Sauvignon Blanc
Beef Wellington	Châteauneuf-du-Pape	*Feta*	Gewürztraminer
	Crozes Hermitage		Greek Red
Bouillabaisse	Dry Rosé	*Gorgonzola*	Alsatian Muscat
	California Fumé Blanc		Sauternes
	Sauvignon Blanc		Tokay
	Dry Tavel Rosé or Spanish Rosé		Austrian Gewürztraminer
Caesar Salad	California Chardonnay	*Gruyère*	Light Red Bardolino
			Dry Swiss or Austrian White
Carpaccio (beef)	Champagne		Pinot Gris
	Chianti Classico Riserva		
		Mozzarella	Dolcetto d'Alba
Caviar	Chilled Vodka		
	Champagne	*Muenster*	German Trocken
			Gewürztraminer

Parmesan	Barolo	Consommé	Dry Sherry
Roquefort	Côtes du Rhône Red Sauternes Barsac	Curry	Chilled Lager New World Chardonnay Anjou Rosé White Bordeaux
Stilton	Vintage or Late-bottled Port		Riesling
Taleggio	Mature Chianti Classico		

Desserts

		Apple Pie	Sweet German wine Sauternes
Cheese Fondue	Pinot Gris		
Cheese Pie	New World Chardonnay	Cakes	Sherry Tokaji (for coffee and vanilla
Cheese Soufflé	Champagne	flavour)	
Chicken		Chocolate Cake	Orange Muscat
		Christmas Pudding	Iberian Muscatel
Roast	Chablis Pouilly-Fumé	Creams & Custards	Sauternes
Stir-fry	Alsatian Riesling	Crème Brûlée	Champagne Sauternes Tokay
Fricassee	Italian Chardonnay		Malmsey Madeira
Chili	Very cold Lager		
Clams	Champagne Chablis Premier Cru Sancerre	Crème Caramel	Loupiac Sauternes
		Fresh Fruit	Muscat Sparkling Wines
Club Sandwich	Light, White Zinfandel		Sauternes

Fruit & Cream Cakes	Sweet, Sparkling Vouvray	Zabaglione	Marsala
Fruit Flans	Coteaux du Layon Sauternes Barsac	Eggs	Champagne
		Escargots	Beaujolais Villages White Macon-Villages
Fruit Salad	Sweet Sherry Asti California Muscat Canelli Clairette de Die	Fish	
		Bass	Dry Reisling
Lemon Meringue Pie	Ice Wine	Cod	Chablis Mersault
Meringue	Sparkling Moscato Late Harvest Riesling Sauternes Sweet Vouvray	Crab (cold)	Reisling Grand Cru Chablis Champagne
		Crab (soft-shell)	Chardonnay
Mille-feuille	Champagne	Crayfish	Sancerre Pouilly-Fumé
Mince Pies	Asti		
Nuts	Port Madeira Mature Sauternes Iberian Moscatel	Frito Misto	Frascati
		Gravlax	Grand Cru Chablis New World Chardonnay
Sponge Cake	Mature Sauternes Port Madeira	Haddock	Chardonnay
		Halibut	Muscadet Pinot Grigio Alsace Pinot Blanc
Strawberries & Cream	Champagne		
Tiramisu	Port		

Lobster	Champagne New World Chardonnay White Burgundy Sauvignon Blanc	Trout	Chablis
		Tuna	Chardonnay
Lobster Salad	Reisling	Tuna Carpaccio	Chardonnay
Mussels	Chablis Sancerre Aligoté Muscadet Sèvre et Maine	Turbot	Chassagne-Montrachet
		Foie Gras	Sauternes (lightly chilled) Barsac Fine Vintage Champagne Pinot Gris Alsace Gewürztraminer
Salmon (fresh)	Puligny-Montrachet Chassagne-Montrachet Chardonnay		
		Grapefruit	Port
Salmon Carpaccio	Chardonnay	Guacamole	New World Chardonnay
Sashimi	Sake Scotch	Ham	Pinot Gris
		Hollandaise	New World Chardonnay
Scallops	Chablis Champagne	Hors d'oeuvres	Sancerre Red Bordeaux
Snapper	Sauvignon Blanc		
Sole	White Burgundy White Bordeaux Young Blanc de Blanc Champagne Muscadet Pinot Blanc d'Alsace	Hummus	Gewürztraminer
		Mayonnaise	Sauvignon Blanc Verdicchio
Swordfish	Chardonnay		

Meat		
Barbecues	Zinfandel	
Calf's Liver	Pinot Noir	
	Côte-Rôtie	
Chicken Liver	Zinfandel	
Coq au Vin	Red Burgundy	
Duck	Young Bordeaux	
	Mature Cru Beaujolais	
Duck à l'Orange	Red Burgundy	
	Châteauneuf-du-Pape	
	Red Rioja	
Goose	Young Bordeaux	
	Mature Cru Beaujolais	
Hamburger	Beaujolais	
	Chilean Cabernet Sauvignon	
	California Merlot	
Kidneys	California Cabernet	
	Rioja	
	Châteauneuf-du-Pape	
Lamb	Red Bordeaux	
	Cabernet	
	Mature Chianti	
	Red Rioja	
Meatballs	Zinfandel	

Osso Bucco	St.-Émilion
	Pomerol
	California Cabernet
Pheasant	Crozes-Hermitage
	Châteauneuf-du-Pape
Pork	White Burgundy
	Chardonnay
	Beaujolais
Rabbit	Red Bordeaux
	New World Chardonnay
	Chianti Classico
Roast Beef	Red Bordeaux
	Australian Cabernet
	Rhône
Roast Chicken	Chablis
	Pouilly-Fumé
Sausage	Italian, Australian, Spanish Reds
Steak, Grilled	Bordeaux
	New World Cabernet Sauvignon
Steak au Poivre	Cabernet
	Zinfandel
	Rhône Shiraz
Steak Tartare	Beaujolais
Steak, T-Bone	Barolo
	Cabernet

Stew	Red Bordeaux	Meat	Merlot
	Zinfandel		Chianti Classico
			Montepulciano d'Abruzzo
Stir-fry Chicken	Alsatian Riesling		
		Pesto	Sauvignon Blanc
Sweetbreads	Dry German Riesling		Cabernet Sauvignon
			Tyrol Merlot
Turkey	Chardonnay		
	Rosé	Primavera	Piedmont Gavi
			Sicilian White
Venison	California Cabernet Sauvignon		
	Barolo	Seafood	Sauvignon Blanc
	Cabernet Shiraz		Soave
		Tomato	Zinfandel
Melon	Port		Valpolicella
			Bardolino
Oysters (raw)	Non-Vintage Champagne		Dolcetto d'Alba
	Chablis Premier Cru		
	Sancerre		
	Pouilly-Fumé	Paté	
		Chicken Liver	Light Pomerol
Oysters (cooked)	Sauvignon Blanc		Sherry
	Semillon		Chenin Blanc
	Chardonnay		
		Country	Australian Shiraz
Paella	Red Rioja		
		Duck	Chianti Classico
Pasta			Loire Red
			Sancerre
Aglio e Olio	Pinot Grigio		
		Other	Macon-Villages
Cream	Italian Chardonnay		Graves
			Fumé Blanc

Pizza	Chianti	*Niçoise*	Provence Rosé
			California Sauvignon Blanc
Prosciutto	California Zinfandel		
	Riesling	*Tabouli*	Alsace Muscat
Quiches	Beaujolais-Villages	*Tzatziki*	Cypriot Dry Whites
	Pinot Gris		
	Sauvignon Blanc	*Waldorf*	Gewürztraminer
	Chilean Chardonnay		
		Salami	Zinfandel
Ratatouille	Chilled, Dry Rosé		
	Southern French Reds like	Shrimp	Fine Mature Champagne
	Corbières or Minervois		Burgundy
			Bordeaux
			Chardonnay
Risotto			
Marinara	Soave	Smoked Salmon	Riesling
	Frascati		Vintage Champagne
			Vodka
Mushroom	Bardolino		Akvavit
	Valpolicella		
		Smoked Trout	New World Sauvignon Blanc
Primavera	Pinot Grigio		Oaky New World Chardonnay
	Soave		
	Well-chilled Sherry		
		Soufflés	
Saffron Sauce	Chardonnay	*Cheese*	Red Burgundy
	Provence Rosé		Cabernet Sauvignon
Salads		*Fish*	Chardonnay
Caesar	New World Sauvignon Blanc		
		Mushroom	White Bordeaux
Greek	Cypriot Dry White		
		Spinach	Macon-Villages

Soup		
Beef Consommé	Sherry	
	Malt Whisky	
Borscht	Hungarian Tokay	
Carrot Soup	Portuguese Rosé	
Chicken Broth	Sherry	
Chowder, Corn	German Riesling	
Chowder, New England	New World Chardonnay	
Cream of Chicken	Sherry	
	German Trocken Wines	
Fish Soup	Good Beaujolais	
	Provence Rosé	
French Onion	Southern French Reds like Corbières or Fitou	
Gazpacho	Chilled Sherry	
	Lemony, white Rioja	
Lentil	Australian Shiraz-Cabernet Blends	
Lobster Bisque	New World Sauvignon Blanc	
	New World Chardonnay	
Minestrone	Verdicchio	
Mulligatawny	Chilled Lager	

Mushroom	Dry Sherry	
	New World Chenin Blanc	
Pumpkin	Beaujolais	
Tomato	Southern French Reds like Corbières	
Vegetable	Austrian Riesling	
Vichyssoise	White Burgundy	
Watercress	Alsace Riesling	
Tapas	Fino or Manzanilla Sherry	
	Dry White Rioja	
Tapenade	The salty flavour makes this dish a potential wine killer. Try a dry Rosé.	
Taramosalata	New World Sauvignon Blanc	
Terrine (Vegetable)	Young, dry, light, aromatic white wines from the Loire, Alsace or Germany	
Thai Food	Cold Lager	
	New World Sauvignon Blanc	
	Non-Vintage Champagne	
Tomatoes	Robust Chianti (acid in tomatoes is no friend to wine)	

ANNOTATED READING LIST

Imagine you are going to be living on a desert island and can take only ten household management reference books with you—a terrifying prospect, I know. What would they be and why? Below, I've listed the ten I don't think I could ever live without. I have my nose in them often, and when I'm not perusing their pages for guidance, they live in my coveted bookshelf behind my desk. Thank you to the authors who penned them!

The National Trust Manual of Housekeeping:
The Care of Collections in Historic Houses Open to the Public
The National Trust, Butterworth-Heinemann, 2005.
I adore this book because it teaches you how to clean and manage correctly, but then explains why you perform a technique in a particular way and why it makes a difference. This is not a book for amateur housecleaners but for professionals in the domestic industry.

Home Comforts: The Art and Science of Keeping House
Cheryl Mendelson, Scribner, 1999.
This book on housekeeping will interest anyone with a penchant for details.

Laundry: The Home Comforts Book of Caring for Clothes and Linens
Cheryl Mendelson, Scribner, 2005.
Laundry is one of my all-time favourite subjects. This is a wonderful resource for those who work in fashion, or for anyone wanting to care properly for clothes.

Difford's Guide to Cocktails #7: Over 2250 Cocktails
Simon Difford, Sauce Guides Limited, 2008.
I can't imagine any professionally run household without this book. It includes recipes and great information about local customs regarding alcoholic beverages.

Le répertoire de la cuisine:
The World Renowned Classic Used by the Experts
Louis Saulnier, translated by E. Brunet,
Barron's Educational Series, 1977.
When I worked at the famous Fenton's Restaurant in Toronto, Executive Chef Werner Basin

introduced me to this book, and the value of understanding and correctly using classical terms. I remember the very first thing I learned was that "Eggs Florentine" meant eggs cooked with spinach. This is not a recipe book, but a list of French terms. A must-have for household professionals or cooking enthusiasts.

Mastering the Art of French Cooking, 50th Anniversary Edition
Julia Child, Louisette Bertholle and Simone Beck,
Alfred A. Knopf, 2001.
There is no better cook or teacher than Julia Child. I had the honour of meeting her three times and each was better than the last. You could spend the rest of your life with only this one book and eat well every single day.

The Joy of Cooking, 75th Anniversary Edition
Irma S. Rombauer, Marion Rombauer Becker
and Ethan Becker, Scribner, 2006.
This book is one that anybody can follow, but more
important, it gives you the first steps of cooking successfully on your own. I truly believe that this is the best foolproof, go-to cookbook. And, even better, it's aimed at the North American market so you'll be able to find any of the ingredients mentioned.

Essentials of Classic Italian Cooking
Marcella Hazan, Alfred A. Knopf, 1992.
I do not know of a better Italian cookbook author than Marcella Hazan. I have prepared countless recipes from her book over the years and never had a recipe go wrong. Count on this book for good family-style cooking, or masterful entertaining.

Amy Vanderbilt's Complete Book of Etiquette:
The Guide to Gracious Living
Amy Vanderbilt, Doubleday, 1958.
This is my personal bible. I have such respect for Amy Vanderbilt and believe she truly understood etiquette. And despite this being a vintage book from the 1950s, the information remains relevant today. It might be difficult to find a copy, as this edition is out of print, but keep your eyes peeled—it's worth it!

Le protocole: instrument de communication 2e edition
Louis Dussault, Protos, 2003.
Available only in French, this is the best guide for Canadian diplomatic protocol. It is magnificently conceived and written.

Honor & Respect: The Official Guide to Names, Titles, and Forms of Address
Robert Hickey, Protocol School of Washington, 2008.
This book on American, Canadian and international protocol of names, titles and forms of address is detailed, accurate and incredibly helpful. Among many topics, it covers how to address dignitaries and VIPs in writing and in person. I often give this book as a gift to people who work in the service industry. Professional households and corporate executive assistants need this on their desk or in their library.

ACKNOWLEDGEMENTS

I consider myself lucky for the family, friends and colleagues who have, in all sorts of ways, contributed and helped me with this book. Thank you for everything you have done. I am eternally grateful to the following people:

Marcus L.H. Dearn	Sean Davoren	Matthew Haack
Scott B. Munden	Pamela Eyring	Michael T. Wright II
Judy Muromoto	Marilyn Denis	Mrs. Erma Jeni
Gabriella Depesthy	Charlotte Empey	Mr. John Myers
Debby Atkinson	Olivier Crémont	Dr. Barbara C. Eastman
John Robertson	Chris Young	Bert Browne
Nita Pronovost	Benjamen Douglas	Bonnie Aprile
Zoe Maslow	Jan Longone	Elliot Gilbert
Robert McCullough	Lilana Novakovich	Gilberto J. Bojaca
Brad Martin	Michelle Crespi	Greg Kelley
Kristin Cochrane	David Barette	Julie Fredette
Scott Richardson	Arthur Baca, Jr.	Matt Binkley
Cathy Paine	Gary Armstrong	Nicole Adams
Lindsay Paterson	Robert Hickey	Derek Humble
Dan Mozersky	Diane Brown	Madame Viviene Neri
Lolly Mozersky	Sean Kelley	M. Philipe Neri
Roanne Goldsman	Julie MacLeod-Haum	Madame Rosemary McCallum
Naomi Strasser	Susan Taylor	Shelagh Aizlewood

INDEX

Italicized page numbers refer to illustrations.

cocktail napkins with, 128; crackers or bread with, 128; how to serve, 125-28

Chef, 10, 10, 15, 18, 23, 114, 226, 229; duties of, 15, 115, 226

China (nation), 48, 188

China (tableware), 96-98; choosing, 89-90, 91, 96; plates, 96, 96; coffee and tea service, 97, 97, serving dishes, 97, 97-98, 98

Chopsticks, 149, 168-69; placement of in table setting, 105

Cleaning, 180-81; calendar for, 183; how to clean a room, 184; tools and supplies for, 181, 184, 186; use of chemicals in, 179, 184; see also Housecleaning, Deep cleaning

Clothing: how to fold, 213-15; types of hangers for, 209-10

Coffee, 75-76, 93; varieties of, 75, 75-76

Cook, see Chef

Crystal, how to clean, 137-38

Cutlery, 99-100, 105, 118, 149; choosing, 90; how to clean, 140-41; how to store, 141; silver, 141; stainless steel, 141

Cutlery, proper use of, 154, 156, 160-65, 167-75; American

style, 162, 163, 170; Continental style, 163, 164, 170; the dinner knife and fork, 160-61

Cutlery, types of, 99-101; for dessert, 163-64; for escargot, 174; for fish, 165, 166, 174; forks, 99, 119; knives, 99, 118, 149; serving utensils, 100-101; spoons, 100, 118, 167

de la Renta, Oscar, xxii

Decoration, periods and styles of: British, 35-36; French, 36; Japanese, 36; Chinese, 37

Deep cleaning, 181, 182, 183, 190, 226; defined, 181

Dishes, care of: in the dishwasher, 138, 140; how to dry, 138, 139; how to wash, 138-40; how to store, 96, 139

Dishwashers, 138; cleaning cutlery in, 140-41; cleaning dishes in, 138, 140; how to load, 140-41; soap for, 140

Downton Abbey, xii, 9, 15, 19, 68

Dress code, 152-53, 154; terms defined, 153

Dusting, 180, 182, 184, 185, 190, 200; and polishes, 200; tools for, 200

Edison, Thomas, 16

Edward VII, King, 6

Electricity, impact of on household management, 16-17

Elizabeth II, Queen, 15

Entertaining, elements of: bar, 129-32; conversation, 155, 158-59; flowers, 88; food, 86; music 88, 119; role played by host/hostess, 85, 87-88, 113, 149, 154-55, 169

Entertaining, etiquette for, 83-143; history of, 83-84; rules for, 84-85, 150-51

Escoffier, Auguste, xix

Estate manager, 226

Etiquette: between men and women, 54-55, 57, 59, 65, 157-58; in a business setting, 57, 59, 62, 63, 65, 90, 148, 149, 153, 154; for carrying, serving a tray, 55-56; with cars, 64-66; at court, 83; defined, xvi, xvii; at doors and doorways, 53-55; for greetings, 52-53; for handshaking, 60-62; for introductions, 48-49, 51-52, 58-60; purpose and value of, xv, xvi, 84; at the table, 147-49; Western compared to Asian, 51, 61, 62; see also Entertaining, etiquette for

Farmer's Almanac, 188

Finger bowl, use of, 170

Finishing school, 226

Fire, how to build, 66-67

Fish knife and fork, history of, 166

Flatware, *see* Cutlery

Floors, washing and drying, 180, 186, 191, 194-99, 204; ceramic, 197; cork, 198; hand-drying, 196-97; hardwood, 198; laminate, 199; marble or stone, 199; tools and supplies for, 194, 195, 196-99

Food and wine pairings, 231–238

Foods, hard-to-eat, 169-75; *see also* Sushi, how to eat

Footman, xxi, 5, 9, 10, 12, 22, 46, 226, 232; duties of, 12, 226

Forms of address, 28

Furniture, how to safely move, 199

Gentleman's gentleman, 226; role of, 226

Gift-wrapping, 76-79

Gifts, for host/hostess, 152

Glassware, 102, 102, 131, 135; crystal, 91, 137-38; how to clean, 137-38; types of, 102

Gosford Park, 27

Governess, 46, 227

Greeting line, staff, how to set up, 18-19, 19

Greetings, etiquette for, 52-53

Guest books, 160

Hallboy, xxi, 10, 12-13; duties of, 12-13

Handshake, etiquette for, 60-62; and transmission of viruses, 62

Hopkins, Anthony, 42

Hotel industry, xix, 47, 108, 187, 189

House steward, 10, 10, 11; duties of, 11

House cleaning, 227; defined, 180-81; and surface cleaning, 230; *see also* Deep cleaning

Household management: history of, xviii-xxi; in Edwardian era, 3-4, 6, 9-18, 20, 21, 108, 138, 179, 188; and introduction of electricity, 16-17, 26; in Victorian era, 3-4, 5-6, 8, 21, 108, 138, 179

Household manager, 47, 227; role of, 227

Household Procedures Manual, 227

Housekeeper, 9, 10, 10, 13, 22, 24, 46, 180, 187, 227, 228; duties of, 13, 180, 227; and the "housekeeper's eye," 184, 185, 227

Housekeeper, executive, 227 228

Housekeeping, 180, 190, 203, 229; defined, 180; and detailing, 180, 185, 203, 227, 228; rules for, 182; and tidying, 180, 190, 227, 228

Introductions, etiquette for, 48-49, 58-60; and bowing/ curtseying, 51-52

Ironing (clothing), 205-208; how to iron shirts, 205-206; laundry symbols for, 208; temperature chart for, 207

Ironing (newspapers), 33-34

Japan, etiquette in, 149, 168

Jennings, Sarah (Duchess of Marlborough), 119

Johnson, Dorothea, 59

Kelly, Greg, 179, 200

Kitchen: choosing appliances for, 203, 204; how to clean, 181, 203-204

Kitchen maid, 10, 18, 228; duties of, 18, 228

Lady's maid, 9, 10, 13-14, 22, 228; duties of, 13, 228

Land steward, 10, 10, 11, 228; duties of, 11, 228

ABOUT THE AUTHOR

Charles is the founder of Charles MacPherson
Associates Inc. and has over twenty-four years of experience
in household management. In 2009, Charles opened North
America's only registered school for butlers and household
managers in Toronto. Throughout his career, Charles has
consulted for both residential and hospitality clients in
Canada, the United States, the United Kingdom, South Africa,
the Middle East and China. He is an expert in the areas of
staffing, training and planning, and is recognized as a world
authority in the household management and butler fields.
Charles has trained the butler departments of the Four
Seasons Hotel in Shanghai, the staff of the *Queen Mary II* and
the staff of Fouquet's Barrière Hôtel in Paris—in addition to
training the household staff for numerous celebrities.

Visit Charles at **www.charlesmacpherson.com**.